3RD Edition

BEST ☗ TENT
Camping

NEW MEXICO

YOUR CAR-CAMPING GUIDE TO SCENIC BEAUTY, THE SOUNDS
OF NATURE, AND AN ESCAPE FROM CIVILIZATION

For Andy, my companion in adventure

Best Tent Camping: New Mexico
Copyright © 2008 and 2014 by Monte R. Parr
Copyright © 2021 by Amaris Feland Ketcham
All rights reserved
Printed in the United States of America
Published by Menasha Ridge Press
Distributed by Publishers Group West
Third edition, first printing

Library of Congress Cataloging-in-Publication Data

Names: Ketcham, Amaris Feland, author.
Title: Best tent camping: New Mexico : your car-camping guide to scenic beauty, the sounds of nature, and an
    escape from civilization / Amaris Feland Ketcham.
Description: 3rd edition. | Birmingham, AL : Menasha Ridge Press, an imprint of AdventureKEEN, [2021]
Identifiers: LCCN 2020042790 (print) | LCCN 2020042791 (ebook) | ISBN 9781634042796 (pbk.) |
    ISBN 9781634042802 (ebook)
Subjects: LCSH: Camping—New Mexico—Guidebooks. | Camp sites, facilities, etc.—New Mexico—Guidebooks. |
    New Mexico—Guidebooks.
Classification: LCC GV191.42.N6 K48 2021 (print) | LCC GV191.42.N6 (ebook) | DDC 647.94209789—dc23
LC record available at https://lccn.loc.gov/2020042790
LC ebook record available at https://lccn.loc.gov/2020042791

Project editor: Holly Cross
Cover and book design: Jonathan Norberg
Maps: Steve Jones and Amaris Feland Ketcham
Photos: Amaris Feland Ketcham, except as noted
Copy editor: Ritchey Halphen
Proofreader: Emily Beaumont
Indexer: Rich Carlson

MENASHA RIDGE PRESS
An imprint of AdventureKEEN
2204 First Ave. S., Ste. 102
Birmingham, AL 35233
800-443-7227, fax 205-326-1012

Visit menasharidge.com for a complete listing of our books and for ordering information. Contact us at our website, at facebook.com/menasharidge, or at twitter.com/menasharidge with questions or comments. To find out more about who we are and what we're doing, visit blog.menasharidge.com.

Cover photo: On the road to Rio Chama Campground (see page 70); © Amaris Feland Ketcham
Inset: Paliza Family Campground (see page 64); © Amaris Feland Ketcham

For the latest coronavirus news and updates pertaining to the campgrounds in this book, please check the "Contact" listings in the campground profiles. For general information about the coronavirus in New Mexico, see cv.nmhealth.org.

3RD Edition

BEST TENT
Camping

NEW MEXICO

YOUR CAR-CAMPING GUIDE TO SCENIC BEAUTY, THE SOUNDS
OF NATURE, AND AN ESCAPE FROM CIVILIZATION

Amaris Feland Ketcham
Prior edition by Monte Parr

MENASHA RIDGE PRESS
Your Guide to the Outdoors Since 1982

New Mexico Campground Locator Map

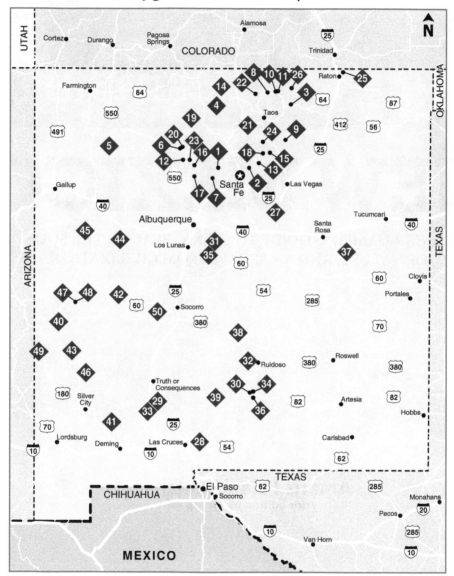

CONTENTS

NORTHERN NEW MEXICO 12

SOUTHEASTERN NEW MEXICO 98

SOUTHWESTERN NEW MEXICO 136

Map Legend

North indicator	Off-map or pinpoint-indication arrow	Individual tent sites, cabins, RV sites, lodges, yurts, and premium deck sites	Group camping sites/areas

Santa Fe ★ Capital	Albuquerque ● City or town	NATIONAL FOREST STATE PARK WILDLIFE REFUGE Public lands	Hiking, biking, and equestrian trails

Interstate highways	US highways	State roads	Other roads

Road direction	Dirt/gravel road	River or stream — Chestnut Branch	Lake or pond — Stump Lake

Amphitheater	Equestrian parking	Picnic pavilion
Archery range	Fee/registration station	Playground
Basketball court	Fire tower	■ Point of interest
Beach	Fishing pier	Primitive toilet
Boat parking	Gate	Ranger station/office
Boat ramp	Horseshoe pit	Recycling station
Boat rental	Information	Restroom
Bridge	Laundry	Showers
Bridle tie-off	Marina	Shelter
Campground	Minigolf	Store
Canoe/kayak entry	Movie theater	Swimming area
Concessions	Observation platform	Trash disposal
Covered bridge	Overlook	Volleyball court
Dam	Parking	Water access
Disc golf	Pet area	Water disposal
Dump station	Phone access	Wheelchair access
Equestrian campsite	Picnic area	

ACKNOWLEDGMENTS

My deepest gratitude to Andy Carey, who had never camped in a campground before I invited him to City of Rocks State Park. He quickly adapted from archaeology dig sites and public-land primitive camping, and he was outstanding company for many of the explorations written about here. Thank you, too, to the many others who joined me for short journeys all across the state—including my mother, who fell in love with the Zuni sandstone at El Morro. I am grateful for my little snowshoe cat, Yuki, who always reminded me to take frequent writing breaks to play.

Thank you to the many befuddled campground hosts who answered my questions and let me walk around photographing various sites. Many thanks to the rangers and administrators of our public lands, who uphold their mission to introduce so many to the joys and wonders of nature. Everyone at Menasha Ridge Press and AdventureKEEN has been great to work with. I'd also like to thank the friendly folks in the town of Reserve, New Mexico, who stopped to help when I had both a flat tire and a busted spare.

I would like to acknowledge that these campgrounds and public lands sit on the traditional homelands of the original peoples of New Mexico—Pueblo, Navajo, and Apache—who have deep connections to the land and have remained stewards throughout the generations.

Unfortunately, I cannot say that "no animals were harmed in the making of this book." Just outside of Canjilon Lakes, a buck in velvet bounded out of the sagebrush into the side of my car and died quickly by the side of the road. I dreamed about his spirit many nights since, and so I would like to acknowledge him and wish him peace.

—Amaris Feland Ketcham

PREFACE

The first time I camped in New Mexico, I pitched a borrowed tent near Chama between a small, man-made lake and the Colorado border. I spent my days wandering through ferns and aspen; my nights, stargazing while coyotes sang. At the lake, a boy proudly showed me the large rainbow trout he'd just caught, and I hiked on, admiring wildflowers while monsoon clouds gathered in the afternoon sky. The forest held many surprises: I chanced upon a rafter of turkeys one day and an old hunting blind the next. Toasting marshmallows over the campfire to make s'mores, I decided to add a roasted green chile and found an instant favorite, decadent dessert. I was a teenager, new to camping, but Chama had me hooked.

I couldn't wait until my next adventure sleeping under the Milky Way. New Mexico has so many places to explore—badlands, canyons, mesas, mountains, prairies, sand dunes, salt flats, valleys, and volcanic escarpments—you could plan a lifetime of weekend trips. In addition to situating yourself within a landscape of geologic masterpieces, camping here also places you in touch with history and the many cultures that live throughout the state.

I've stumbled upon fossils, ancient pottery sherds, and secret, hidden petroglyphs. Once, camping in the Gila, it was so cold that I shivered most of the night instead of sleeping. In the morning, I watched as my breath rose up in a little cloud, condensed, froze, and snowed back down on my face—I had created my own miniature weather system in my tent. This was such a beautiful moment, and I'd never seen or even imagined anything like it.

Another time, I was hiking out from my campsite at White Sands National Park when a storm started to blow in. The sky turned light gray, and wind lifted the sand. The sky grew indistinguishable from the dunes in these whiteout conditions; the world was white. But our long morning shadows persisted to show us the direction of the sun, and luckily the guideposts also remained visible. Again, I'd never seen anything like it. That's part of what draws me out time and time again: the New Mexican wilderness is full of secrets, surprises, and experiences like nothing you've ever seen. Wanting to share these kinds of experiences with others has fueled much of the research and writing of this book.

Perhaps that's why I've had such a difficult time answering the one question everyone asks after learning that I'm researching campgrounds: "What's your favorite campground?" I have many favorite campgrounds for different kinds of camping experiences—some to admire the stars, to sleep under tall pines, to investigate archaeology sites, or wander trails. People camp for many reasons; others might have their own campgrounds for preferred activities and settings. If you like trout fishing in a rushing river with your tent hidden behind low growth, a bustling campground where kids can make friends at the playground, or pitching a tent among eroded boulders of volcanic tuff that look like a setting from *The Flintstones*, you'll find a great campground in this guide. You'll also find lakeside campgrounds, secluded mountain campgrounds, and campgrounds close to hot springs and climbing routes. I've visited scores of campgrounds in New Mexico and tried to include a variety of the best in this guide.

Unfortunately, not all of the campgrounds I'd wanted to include could be accessed, as a couple were undergoing extensive renovations. It will be exciting to see the improvements that the U.S. Forest Service (USFS) and New Mexico State Parks make to these locations. After these renovations, other campgrounds are scheduled for construction, fees will likely change, and sometimes water wells will be out for a season—check with the appropriate agency before you go.

For the third edition, I've added some sites and thus had to cut some too. A notable addition is **White Sands National Park,** one of our newest national parks. While it's more primitive than the other campgrounds written about here, White Sands is an unparalleled camping experience and one every New Mexico tent camper should experience at least once; you can learn more about it in these pages.

Some sites I cut reluctantly. While they may have offered great historical or geological significance and the areas seemed well worth visiting, the campgrounds may have been better suited to RVs or appeared to have returned to nature. Others were in areas already dense with campgrounds I was profiling, so I decided to add some a little farther afield. Visiting and reviewing campgrounds has taken me all across the state, into the national forests and grasslands, national and state parks, and monuments in the beautiful public lands of New Mexico.

For ease of reference, this guidebook divides the state into three major geographic areas. In **Northern New Mexico,** you'll find campgrounds in the Carson and Santa Fe National Forests, the tail of the Rocky Mountains, spectacular alpine lakes, and ruins of impressive settlements. North of I-40, these campgrounds are sure to impress with their cool summer nights, challenging hikes, and great fishing. From the Manzano Mountains to the home of the real-life Smokey Bear, the **Southeastern New Mexico** campgrounds are a mix of mountains and cacti-covered desert. East of I-25, you can set up your base camp to hike portions of the historic Cloud Climbing Railroad; photograph brilliant autumn colors; or sled in soft, white sand. Camping in **Southwestern New Mexico** might take you into New Mexico's wildest wilderness in the Gila National Forest, fields of lava in El Malpais, or through the plains near the Very Large Array. West of I-25, you can follow the trail of Spanish, appreciate petroglyphs, or hike the incredible Catwalk above Whitewater Canyon, then grab some freshly baked pie or soak in hot springs.

While I've worked hard to collect the most up-to-date information on all of the campgrounds presented in this book, changes are inevitable. It's a good idea to call ahead or check the internet for the most updated information on the campground you plan to visit. (Be aware, for example, that fee increases are likely to occur in the next few years at USFS campgrounds.) I would appreciate knowing about any noteworthy changes you may come across; you can contact me at amarisketcham.com. In the meantime, I hope this book helps you find a new favorite campground, stay hooked on the outdoors, or have an experience you never could have imagined.

—A. F. K.

BEST CAMPGROUNDS

BEST FOR DARK-SKY EXPERIENCES

BEST FOR DESERT CAMPING

BEST FOR FISHING

The half-moon shape of Pueblo Bonito at Chaco Culture National Historical Park lines up perfectly with the cardinal directions (*see page 26*).

BEST FOR GEOLOGIC FEATURES

BEST FOR HIKING

BEST FOR FAMILIES WITH KIDS

BEST FOR SCENIC VISTAS AND PHOTOGRAPHY

BEST FOR SOAKING IN HOT SPRINGS

A tree struggling to survive in Water Canyon takes on a sculptural appearance (*see page 167*).

INTRODUCTION

HOW TO USE THIS GUIDEBOOK

Welcome to *Best Tent Camping: New Mexico*. Whether you're new to camping or you've been sleeping in your portable shelter for decades of outdoor adventures, please review the following information. It explains how this book is organized and how you can make the best use of it.

Some text on the following pages applies to all books in the Best Tent Camping series. Where this isn't the case, such as descriptions of weather and wildlife, the author has provided information specific to the area covered in this particular book.

THE RATINGS AND RATINGS CATEGORIES

The author personally experienced dozens of campgrounds and campsites to select the top 50 locations in New Mexico. Within that universe of 50 sites, the author then ranked each one in the six categories described below. A tough grader, the author awarded few five-star ratings, but each campground in this guidebook is superlative in its own way—for example, a site that rates only one star in a particular category may merit five stars in another category. In every case, the star-rating system is a handy tool to help you pinpoint the campground that will fit your personal requirements.

★★★★★   The site is **ideal** in that category.

★★★★   The site is **exemplary** in that category.

★★★   The site is **very good** in that category.

★★   The site is **above average** in that category.

★   The site is **acceptable** in that category.

BEAUTY

Beauty, of course, is in the eye of the beholder, but panoramic views or proximity to a lake or river earn especially high marks. A campground that blends in well with the environment scores well, as do areas with remarkable wildlife or geology. Well-kept vegetation and nicely laid-out sites also up the ratings.

PRIVACY

The number of sites in a campground, the amount of screening between them, and physical distance from one another are decisive factors for the privacy ratings. Other considerations include the presence of nearby trails or day-use areas, and proximity to a town or city that would invite regular day-use traffic and perhaps compromise privacy.

SPACIOUSNESS

The size of the tent spot, its proximity to other tent spots, and whether or not it is defined or bordered from activity areas are the key considerations. The highest ratings go to sites that allow the tent camper to comfortably spread out without overlapping neighboring sites or picnic, cooking, or parking areas.

QUIET

Criteria for this rating include several touchstones: the author's experience at the site, the nearness of roads, the proximity of towns and cities, the probable number of RVs, the likelihood of noisy all-terrain vehicles or boats, and whether a campground host is available or willing to enforce the quiet hours. Of course, one set of noisy neighbors can deflate a five-star rating into a one-star (or no-star), so the latter criterion—campground enforcement—was particularly important in the author's evaluation in this category.

SECURITY

How you determine a campground's security will depend on who you view as the greater risk: other people or the wilderness. The more remote the campground, the less likely you are to run into opportunistic crime but the harder it is to get help in case of an accident or dangerous wildlife confrontation. Ratings in this category take into consideration whether there is a campground host or resident park ranger, proximity of other campers' sites, how much day traffic the campground receives, how close the campground is to a town or city, and whether there is cell phone reception or some type of phone or emergency call button.

CLEANLINESS

A campground's appearance often depends on who was there right before you and how your visit coincides with the maintenance schedule. In general, higher marks went to those campgrounds with hosts who cleaned up regularly. The rare case of odor-free toilets also gleaned high marks. At unhosted campgrounds, criteria included trash receptacles and evidence that sites were cleared and that signs and buildings were kept repaired. Markdowns for the campground were not given for a single visitor's garbage left at a site, but old trash in the shrubbery and along trails, indicating infrequent cleaning, did secure low ratings.

THE CAMPGROUND PROFILE

Here's where you'll find the nitty-gritty details. Not only is the property described, but readers can also get a general idea of the recreational opportunities available—what's in the area and perhaps suggestions for activities nearby.

THE CAMPGROUND LOCATOR MAP AND MAP LEGEND

To find the best campground in a specific part of the state, begin with the New Mexico Campground Locator Map (page iv), which shows you where all 50 campgrounds are located. Each campground's number appears not only on the locator map but also in the table of contents on the facing page and on each campground profile's first page. A legend that details the symbols found on the campground-layout maps (see next section) appears immediately following the table of contents, on page vii.

CAMPGROUND-LAYOUT MAPS

Each profile contains a detailed map of campground sites, internal roads, facilities, and other key items.

GPS CAMPGROUND-ENTRANCE COORDINATES

We provide each campground's entrance location in latitude–longitude format, expressed in degrees and decimal minutes. For example, the GPS coordinates for Bandelier National Monument: Juniper Family Campground (page 13) are as follows:

N35° 47.764' W106° 16.504'

To convert GPS coordinates from degrees, minutes, and seconds to the above degrees and decimal minutes, divide the seconds by 60. For more on GPS technology, visit usgs.gov.

WEATHER

Maybe you've heard that New Mexico enjoys sunshine over 300 days a year, or that if you don't like the weather, wait 10 minutes and then check it again. While I agree that the weather is generally pleasant, camping in each season and region can bring its own challenges.

Spring is a great time to explore camping in the desert and witness the cactus blooming in a veritable color wheel of electric hues. Expect highs in the 70s and nighttime lows in the 40s. Watch for high winds that can create dust storms that completely obscure roadways. In late May, campgrounds at elevations in the northern part of the state open; check the weather before you go, as late hailstorms and snowstorms are common. Summers tend to be hot, with comfortably cool nights. Even when the temperature breaks into triple digits, it will cool off rapidly once the sun sets.

The higher in elevation you go, the cooler it will be both day and night. Remember that UV rays are stronger at high altitudes and you may need sunscreen with a greater SPF protection. Monsoon season usually begins in late June and lasts until early September. Once the rain starts, the temperature can drop rapidly. Afternoon rains may affect access on gravel and dirt roads; watch for washes where roads dip. Flash flooding can occur even with only a little rain; take precautions while exploring slot canyons and dry arroyos, and get to safety at the first sign of a storm. Forests can also be dangerous during flash floods, especially in areas recently affected by fires or with standing dead trees from insect infestations and disease.

Autumn is a wonderful time of year to camp anywhere in the state. Aspens turn bright yellow and elks bugle day and night in the mountains. Most campgrounds in the mountains close in October, but they may still have walk-in availability for hunters. The days are cool, with temperatures in the 70s and 80s, while nights can be chilly in the 40s. Southern New Mexico booms with snowbirds in the winter. The long nights provide ample opportunity for stargazing and telling stories over a campfire. Daytime temperatures will be in the 50s, while it will drop just below freezing at night. Some campgrounds in the mountains might stay open, with opportunities to ski, snowshoe, or ice-fish during the day.

FIRST AID KIT

A useful first aid kit may contain more items than you might think necessary. The following are just the basics. Prepackaged kits in waterproof bags are available. As a preventive measure, always take along sunscreen and insect repellent. Even though quite a few items are listed here, they pack down into a small space:

- Adhesive bandages
- Antibiotic ointment (such as Neosporin)
- Antihistamine (such as Benadryl), for mild allergies
- Antiseptic or disinfectant (such as Betadine or hydrogen peroxide)
- Aspirin, acetaminophen (Tylenol), or ibuprofen (Advil)
- Butterfly-closure bandages
- Comb and tweezers (for removing ticks from your skin)
- Elastic bandages or joint wraps
- Epinephrine (EpiPen), for serious allergies (e.g., to bee stings)
- Gauze (one roll and six 4-by-4-inch compress pads)
- LED flashlight or headlamp
- Matches or lighter
- Mirror (for signaling passing aircraft)
- Moleskin/Spenco 2nd Skin
- Pocketknife or multipurpose tool
- Waterproof first aid tape
- Whistle (if you get lost or hurt)

FLORA AND FAUNA PRECAUTIONS

BLACK BEARS An estimated 5,000–6,000 black bears live in New Mexico, mostly residing in the same forests and mountain ranges that make for popular campgrounds. You've probably heard that a fed bear is a dead bear. The best way to protect bears and to keep them out of your campsite is to lock away your food at night, including dog food, and to maintain a tidy camp. Wash dishes after you cook, and store food in your car, in provided bear boxes, or strung high up in a tree. Don't leave scented or flavored items such as chewing gum, toothpaste, baby wipes, deodorant, or the like in your tent overnight—they smell like food to bears.

If you see a bear, remain calm. Don't run. Make yourself look larger by raising your arms and make noise. Do not come between a mother and her cubs. You can find bear spray at most camping retailers, and you'll want to consider carrying some with you as you hike.

MOSQUITOES Camping in clouds of mosquitoes is never fun, and while they aren't as bad in New Mexico as they are in other states, you may still encounter these pests near streams, lakes, and areas with lots of snowmelt. Mosquitoes may carry West Nile virus or Zika in some parts of the state. Pack insect repellent to ward them off.

MOUNTAIN LIONS Sleek and sly, mountain lions are among the local predators you're unlikely to meet up close and personal. Blending in easily with the landscape, this tawny large cat is more likely to see you before you ever see it. An estimated 2,500 mountain lions call the New Mexican wilderness home. Check with camp hosts and local rangers about recent sightings. If there has been a mountain lion in the area, avoid going for trail runs at sunrise and sunset, stay in groups, and keep your pets close. If you see a mountain lion, don't turn and run—this may trigger its feline instincts to chase. As with bears, try to make yourself look larger by raising your arms and make noise.

PLAGUE AND HANTAVIRUS New Mexico may be unique in these two health hazards posed by contact with rodents. While plague is rare, it isn't an illness relegated to history textbooks; about half of all US cases each year come from New Mexico. You can contract the plague from fleas that have previously bitten infected rodents. Dogs and cats are also susceptible.

Hantavirus pulmonary syndrome, a severe and potentially fatal respiratory disease, is likewise transmitted by infected rodents. The virus can become aerosolized through urine, droppings, or saliva—particularly from deer mice. While a majority of cases reported occur in the northwestern corner of the state, many counties have reported cases. Between 1975 and 2018, New Mexico reported 117 cases, 49 of which were fatal.

It's best not to feed or attempt to pet chipmunks, ground squirrels, and other rodents, no matter how cute they may look as they beg for food. You may also think twice before entering small caves with evidence of pack-rat dens or rodent burrows.

For more information, visit the New Mexico Department of Health's website, nmhealth.org.

POISON IVY, OAK, AND SUMAC Luckily, at many campgrounds in New Mexico, these poisonous plants won't be an issue; that said, you're most likely to find them near streams, rivers, and other well-watered areas. Recognizing poison ivy, oak, and sumac and avoiding contact with them are the most effective ways to prevent their painful, itchy rashes.

Poison ivy ranges from a thick, tree-hugging vine to a shaded ground cover, 3 leaflets to a leaf; poison oak occurs as either a vine or shrub, with 3 leaflets as well; and poison sumac flourishes in swampland, each leaf containing 7–13 leaflets. Urushiol, the oil in these plants, is responsible for the rash. Usually within 12–14 hours of exposure (but sometimes much

Poison ivy   Poison oak   Poison sumac

later), raised lines and/or blisters will appear, accompanied by a terrible itch. Try to refrain from scratching because dirty fingernails can cause an infection.

Wash and dry the rash thoroughly, applying calamine lotion and/or hydrocortisone cream to help relieve the itch. If itching or blistering is severe, seek medical attention. To keep from spreading the misery to someone else, make sure to wash not only exposed parts of your body but also clothes, hiking gear, and pets—it's not unheard of to experience a second outbreak of poison ivy a year after the first due to picking up a backpack or pair of shoes that was never properly cleaned.

SCORPIONS While all scorpions are venomous, the Arizona bark scorpion, found in the southwestern part of New Mexico, is the only local species that can cause serious illness or fatality. This scorpion is drawn to dark, damp places. Shake out shoes, towels, and bedding before using. If you want to look for scorpions at night, bring a black light to search for their glow. While other scorpions may not be fatal—the last recorded scorpion death was in 1968 in Arizona—their stings still hurt and produce swelling. If you do get stung, cleanse and elevate the wound, then apply a cold compress to help lessen any inflammation.

Arizona bark scorpion

SNAKES Snakes emerge from their winter dens in spring, which is probably also when you're getting the camping gear together for a weekend away, and they remain active throughout summer. Venomous snakes have a few recognizable characteristics, including triangular heads, elliptical pupils, and upper jaws with fangs. In New Mexico, the venomous snakes to watch out for are rattlesnakes and coral snakes. Several species of rattlesnakes can be found throughout the state, including western diamond-backed, northern black-tailed, and prairie rattlesnakes. I have seen rattlesnakes while camping in some of the campgrounds listed in this book. Adults tend to be between 2.5 and 4.5 feet long and will rattle their tail if feeling threatened. Their venom is toxic and can be deadly; give them plenty of space if you see one.

Coral snake

Western coral snakes live mostly in the southwest corner of the state. Their venom is highly toxic, but our local species tend to be too small to bite humans. It's easy to confuse the coral snake with the nonvenomous milk snake; luckily, there's a catchy rhyme to help you tell

Milk snake

them apart by their color patterns: "Red touches yellow [coral snake] will kill a fellow; red touches black [milk snake], venom it lacks."

The best rule is to leave all snakes alone, give them a wide berth as you hike past, and make sure any hiking companions (including dogs) do the same. When hiking, stick to well-used trails, and wear over-the-ankle boots and loose-fitting long pants. Do not step or put your hands beyond your range of detailed visibility, and avoid wandering around in the dark. Step onto logs and rocks, never over them, and be especially careful when climbing rocks. Always avoid walking through dense brush or willow thickets. If someone in your party is bitten, thoroughly cleanse the bite and apply a clean dressing. Seek medical attention immediately.

Deer tick

TICKS These bloodsucking arachnids lie in wait in brush along trails until warm-blooded people and animals walk by. Luckily, ticks usually aren't a big problem on trails and campgrounds in New Mexico, but you should still keep an eye out for them year-round. In addition to dining on you, ticks can transmit a variety of diseases. Perform full-body tick checks after hiking and while camping to try to catch them early. Deer ticks and dog ticks may take a while to latch on, which makes them easier to remove, even if they remain difficult to kill. Once a tick has embedded in your skin, use tweezers to detach it.

OTHER ANIMAL THREATS At many campsites, you'll likely hear **coyotes** singing throughout the night. While they tend not to enter the campgrounds themselves, they may grab a pet that strays too far at night. It's unlikely that you'll meet **wolves** or **bobcats** at a campground, but it's good to know you're sharing the woods with them as well. Wolves have been reintroduced in the Gila and are growing in number. **Raccoons** and **ravens** are two notable camp robbers. Both are cunning visitors, adept at stealing unattended food. The same precautions you take to guard against bear encounters at your camp will help keep other hungry animals out as well. Finally, remember to always zip up your tent all the way so spiders, centipedes, and other creepy-crawlies stay out of your sleeping bags.

FIRES

In particularly dry years, many campgrounds may have fire restrictions in place. Check these before you travel so you'll know what type of cooking fuel you can use and whether you can sit around the campfire at night. Always use established fire pits and rings; make sure you have enough water to completely put out your fire before leaving it unattended. You can find restrictions by calling ahead or looking up your intended campsite online; firerestrictions.us/nm is another good resource.

ROADS AND VEHICLES

From dreaded washboard stretches to seasonal closures, it's best to know in advance what the road conditions are as they pertain to the campgrounds in this book. Some are best traversed in a high-clearance vehicle, especially for sites farther from the beaten path. Checking road conditions before loading up your vehicle will make for a more pleasant adventure.

Always keep a road atlas or specific U.S. Forest Service map handy in your car, as GPS and wireless map data can be spotty out in the wilderness. While maps have been provided in this book, they serve only to orient you to the campground and help you find the nearest restroom or water spigot.

PERMITS AND ACCESS

I highly recommend purchasing a federal **Interagency Pass.** These passes, including the annual America the Beautiful Pass and Senior Pass, cover standard entrance and amenity (day-use) fees at lands managed by the National Park Service, U.S. Forest Service, U.S. Fish and Wildlife Service, Bureau of Land Management, Bureau of Reclamation, and U.S. Army Corps of Engineers. Campers enjoy the additional benefit of discounted camping fees—you pay only half of the posted rate at most campgrounds on national lands profiled in this book. This discount also applies if you reserve a site online.

Interagency Passes are free for active military members, people with permanent disabilities, all fourth graders for the duration of the school year through the following summer, and those who log at least 250 volunteer hours with the public-land agencies listed above. The America the Beautiful Pass costs $80, is valid for one year, and grants access to more than 2,000 federal recreation sites. For folks 62 or older, an $80 Senior Pass remains valid for a lifetime (or unless you lose it, since passes cannot be replaced).

Rather than naming specific passes individually, I've simply indicated in the campground profiles where Interagency Passes are accepted in this book. For more information or to purchase a pass, see nps.gov/planyourvisit/passes.htm, recreation.gov/pass, or store .usgs.gov/pass.

New Mexico State Parks have passes of their own and will not accept an Interagency Pass. At emnrd.state.nm.us, you can select from the following annual passes: $180 for New Mexico residents, $100 for seniors (age 62 or older) or people with disabilities, or $225 for out-of-state visitors. Luckily, these parks will replace a lost pass for only $10.

TENT-CAMPING TIPS

Use the following strategies to plan your perfect camping trip.

CAMPGROUND ETIQUETTE

Here are a few recommendations for creating good vibes with fellow campers and wildlife you encounter.

- **MAKE SURE YOU CHECK IN, PAY YOUR FEE, AND MARK YOUR SITE AS DIRECTED.** Don't make the mistake of grabbing a seemingly empty site that looks more appealing than your site. It could be reserved. If you're unhappy with the site you've selected, check with the campground host for other options.

- **BE SENSITIVE TO THE GROUND BENEATH YOU.** Be sure to place all garbage in designated receptacles or pack it out if none is available. No one likes to see the trash someone else has left behind.

- **IT'S COMMON FOR ANIMALS TO WANDER THROUGH CAMPSITES,** where they may be accustomed to the presence of humans (and our food). An unannounced approach, a sudden movement, or a loud noise startles most animals. A surprised animal can be dangerous to you, to others, and to itself. Give animals plenty of space.

- **PLAN AHEAD.** Know your equipment, your ability, and the area where you are camping—and prepare accordingly. Be self-sufficient at all times; carry necessary supplies for changes in weather or other conditions.

- **BE COURTEOUS TO OTHER CAMPERS, HIKERS, BIKERS, AND ANYONE ELSE YOU ENCOUNTER.**

- **STRICTLY FOLLOW THE CAMPGROUND'S RULES** regarding the building of fires. Never burn trash—the smoke smells horrible, and trash debris in a fire pit or grill is unsightly.

HAPPY CAMPING

There is nothing worse than a bad camping trip, especially because it's so easy to have a great time. To assist with making your outing a happy one, here are some pointers:

- **RESERVE YOUR SITE IN ADVANCE,** especially if it's a weekend or a holiday, or if the campground is wildly popular. Many prime campgrounds require at least a six-month lead time on reservations. Check before you go.

- **PICK YOUR CAMPING BUDDIES WISELY.** A family trip is pretty straightforward, but you may want to reconsider including grumpy Uncle Fred, who doesn't like bugs, sunshine, or marshmallows. After you know who's going, make sure that everyone is on the same page regarding expectations of difficulty (amenities or the lack thereof, physical exertion, and so on), sleeping arrangements, and food requirements.

- **DON'T DUPLICATE EQUIPMENT,** such as cooking pots and lanterns, among campers in your party. Carry what you need to have a good time, but don't turn the trip into a cross-country moving experience.

- **DRESS FOR THE SEASON.** Educate yourself on the temperature highs and lows of the specific part of the state you plan to visit. It may be warm at night in the summer in your backyard, but up in the mountains it can be quite chilly.

- **PITCH YOUR TENT ON A LEVEL SURFACE,** preferably one covered with leaves, pine straw, or grass. Use a tarp or specially designed footprint to thwart ground moisture and to protect the tent floor. Do a little site maintenance, such as picking up the small rocks and sticks that can damage your tent floor and make sleep uncomfortable. If you have a separate tent rainfly but don't think you'll need it, keep it rolled up at the base of the tent in case it starts raining at midnight.

- **CONSIDER TAKING A SLEEPING PAD** if the ground makes you uncomfortable. Choose a pad that is full-length and thicker than you think you might need. This will not only keep your hips from aching on hard ground but will also help keep you warm. A wide range of thin, light, and inflatable pads is available at camping stores, and these are a much better choice than home air mattresses, which conduct heat away from the body and tend to deflate during the night.

- **IF YOU'RE NOT HIKING IN TO A PRIMITIVE CAMPSITE,** there is no real need to skimp on food due to weight. Plan tasty meals and bring everything you will need to prepare, cook, eat, and clean up.

- **IF YOU TEND TO USE THE BATHROOM** multiple times at night, you should plan ahead. Leaving a warm sleeping bag and stumbling around in the dark to find the restroom, whether it be a pit toilet, a fully plumbed comfort station, or just the woods, is no fun. Keep a flashlight and any other accoutrements you may need by the tent door, and know exactly where to head in the dark.

- **STANDING DEAD TREES** and storm-damaged living trees can pose a real hazard to tent campers. These trees may have loose or broken limbs that could fall at any time. When choosing a campsite or even just a spot to rest during a hike, *look up.*

A WORD ABOUT BACKCOUNTRY CAMPING

Following these guidelines will increase your chances for a pleasant, safe, and low-impact interaction with nature.

- **ADHERE TO THE ADAGES** "Pack it in, pack it out" and "Take only pictures, leave only footprints." Practice Leave No Trace camping ethics while in the backcountry.

- **IN NEW MEXICO, ALWAYS CHECK FIRE BANS** when planning your trip. Summer restrictions are frequent. Backpacking stoves are strongly encouraged.

- **HANG FOOD AWAY FROM BEARS** and other animals to prevent them from becoming introduced to (and dependent on) human food. Wildlife learns to associate backpacks and backpackers with easy food sources, thereby influencing their behavior.

- **BURY SOLID HUMAN WASTE IN A HOLE** at least 3 inches deep and at least 200 feet away from trails and water sources; a trowel is basic backpacking equipment. More and more often, however, the practice of burying human waste is being banned. Using a portable latrine (basically a glorified plastic bag, given out by park rangers) may seem unthinkable at first, but it's really no big deal. Just bring an extra-large zip-top bag for additional insurance against structural failures.

VENTURING AWAY FROM THE CAMPGROUND

If you go for a hike, bike ride, or other excursion into the wilderness, keep the following precautions in mind.

- **ALWAYS CARRY FOOD AND WATER,** whether you're planning to go overnight or not. Food will give you energy, help keep you warm, and sustain you in an emergency until help arrives. Bring potable water or treat water by boiling or filtering before drinking from a lake or stream.

- **STAY ON DESIGNATED TRAILS.** Most hikers get lost when they leave the trail. Even on the most clearly marked trails, there is usually a point where you have to stop and consider which direction to head. If you become disoriented, don't panic. As soon as you think you may be off-track, stop, assess your current direction, and then retrace your steps back to the point where you went awry. If you have absolutely no idea how to continue, return to the trailhead the way you came in. Should you become completely lost and have no idea of how to return to the trailhead, remaining in place along the trail and waiting for help is most often the best option for adults and always the best option for children.

- **BE ESPECIALLY CAREFUL WHEN CROSSING STREAMS.** Whether you're fording the stream or crossing on a log, make every step count. If you have any doubt about maintaining your balance on a log, go ahead and ford the stream instead. When fording a stream, use a trekking pole or stout stick for balance and *face upstream as you cross.* If a stream seems too deep to ford, turn back. Whatever is on the other side isn't worth the risk.

- **BE CAREFUL AT OVERLOOKS.** Though these areas may provide spectacular views, they are potentially hazardous. Stay back from the edge of outcrops and be absolutely sure of your footing: a misstep can mean a nasty and possibly fatal fall.

- **KNOW THE SYMPTOMS OF HYPOTHERMIA.** Shivering and forgetfulness are the two most common indicators of this stealthy killer. Hypothermia can occur at any elevation, even in the summer. Wearing cotton clothing puts you especially at risk, because cotton, when wet, wicks heat away from the body. To prevent hypothermia, dress in layers using synthetic clothing for insulation, use a cap and gloves to reduce heat loss, and protect yourself with waterproof, breathable outerwear. If symptoms arise, seek shelter, a fire, hot liquids, and dry clothes or a dry sleeping bag.

- **LIKEWISE, KNOW THE SYMPTOMS OF HYPERTHERMIA,** or abnormally high body temperature. Lightheadedness and weakness are the first two indicators. If you feel these symptoms, find some shade, drink some water, remove as many layers of clothing as practical, and stay put until you cool down. Marching through heat exhaustion leads to heatstroke—which can be fatal. If you should be sweating and you're not, that's the signature warning sign. If you or a hiking partner are experiencing heatstroke, do whatever you can to get cool and find help.

- **TAKE ALONG YOUR BRAIN.** Think before you act. Watch your step. Plan ahead. Avoiding accidents before they happen is the best recipe for a rewarding and relaxing hike.

NORTHERN NEW MEXICO

Rio Grande cutthroat trout and brown trout swim the icy waters of the Rio Santa Barbara *(see page 85).*

⛺ Bandelier National Monument:
JUNIPER FAMILY CAMPGROUND

Beauty ★★★ Privacy ★★ Spaciousness ★★ Quiet ★★★ Security ★★★★ Cleanliness ★★★★

Climb a ladder into a small cave dwelling where you can peer out over the Tyuonyi ruins.

Between 1150 and 1600 C.E., Ancestral Pueblo people dug cliff dwellings into the soft volcanic tuff, carved kivas into the earth, and built freestanding structures in Frijoles Canyon, part of the Bandelier National Monument. Archaeologists have uncovered campsites of hunter-gatherers dating back to 1750 B.C.E., but the canyon was abandoned by the 1500s, before Spanish conquistadores arrived.

The monument boasts some 3,000 archaeological sites, but the impressive Long House and Alcove House are the main attractions for most visitors. On this popular trail, ancient footpaths lead you up stone stairways and through narrow slots along the 800-foot stretch of multistoried stone homes and small cave dwellings. Ladders take you into these hand-carved homes in the cliff, where you can peer out over the Tyuonyi ruins. At the Alcove House, the daring can climb four wooden ladders towering 140 feet above the canyon's floor to see a reconstructed kiva.

The park, however, covers 33,750 acres, so there's much more to explore than one day would allow. Luckily, Juniper Family Campground provides a comfortable place to rest between explorations. This campground doesn't often fill up, so all sites (excluding group

From a nearby overlook, you can see the ruins of Tyuonyi Pueblo on the valley floor of Frijoles Canyon.

KEY INFORMATION

LOCATION: 15 Entrance Rd.,
Los Alamos, NM 87544

CONTACT: Bandelier National Monument,
505-672-3861, ext. 517, nps.gov/band/plan
yourvisit/juniper-family-campground.htm

OPEN: Year-round

SITES: 57, including 2 group sites

EACH SITE HAS: Picnic table, campfire ring
with grill, tent area

WHEELCHAIR ACCESS: Sites 38 and 45

ASSIGNMENT: First-come, first-served;
only the 2 group sites ($35/night) can be
reserved (877-444-6777, recreation.gov
/camping/campgrounds/233395).

REGISTRATION: On-site, payable by credit
card at digital kiosk

AMENITIES: A central restroom with running
water is located at the center of each loop.

PARKING: At sites

FEE: $12/night ($6 with Interagency Pass).
Separate park-entrance fee is $25/vehicle
(free with Interagency Pass).

ELEVATION: 6,660'

RESTRICTIONS

PETS: Allowed on leashes; not permitted
on trails within the park

QUIET HOURS: 10 p.m.–6 a.m.

FIRES: In fire rings only. Firewood is sold
within the campground for $1/log.

ALCOHOL: Permitted

OTHER: Limit of 2 tents, 2 vehicles, and
10 people/site. Not all campground loops
may be open at any given time. Generators
may run 8 a.m.–8 p.m. Dump station is at
the entrance.

---

sites) are first come, first served; the visitor center did warn that the campground fills on holidays, though. Claim an empty site and then pay by credit card at the entry kiosk. If you need to pay with cash, you must go to the visitor center before it closes.

Along Abert's Squirrel Loop are two small group sites that accommodate between 10 and 20 people; these are the only two reservation sites in the campground. A separate group campground 6 miles west, Ponderosa, has two sites that can accommodate a maximum of 50 people. A couple of sites have also been combined: sites 19–20 and 21–23 share tent areas, so I would avoid them unless you're camping with a dear friend.

Whereas Coyote Loop seems to accommodate mostly RVs, Black Bear Loop has a good number of dedicated tent sites. Site 25 is ideal—spacious, with a ponderosa pine shading the picnic table. Junipers shade site 33 well; and though site 17 looks small, it has some neat little tent spaces tucked into junipers. Packrat Lane divides Black Bear Loop and provides walk-in access to sites 34–38. These have parking lots on the north and south ends of the loop.

Each loop has flush toilets and sinks with running water to wash your hands. Wash dishes at your campsite, and use the campers' dump sink to dispose of the water.

Bears are active in the area; use the provided bear boxes and keep a clean campsite. In addition to bears, there may be mice, squirrels, pikas, ringtail cats, and raccoons scavenging the campground for food.

Remember that Bandelier National Monument is part of Ancestral Pueblo lands, and leave all ruins and artifacts as you find them. As the Affiliated Pueblo Committee says, "Spiritually, our ancestors still live here at Bandelier. You see reminders of their presence here—their homes, their kivas, their petroglyphs. As you walk in their footsteps, value the earth beneath you and show everything the same respect we do when we revisit this sacred place."

Access to Bandelier National Monument and the Frijoles Canyon Visitor Center is by shuttle bus only: May 17–October 17, daily, 9 a.m.–3 p.m. The shuttle picks up passengers at the parking lot in the Juniper Family Campground, or you can hike down. Two trails leave from the campground: the Frey Trail descends to the visitor center, and the Main Loop Trail is a dusty, steep trail with lots of switchbacks, so you may prefer taking it down and using the shuttle on the way back, or vice versa. The Tyuonyi Overlook Trail leaves the amphitheater parking area for a 0.75-mile hike to an overlook of Frijoles Canyon and Tyuonyi Pueblo. Inside the park, there are 70 miles of hiking trails. The Upper Frijoles Falls Trail is worth a visit.

If you'd like to skip the campground, you can backcountry-camp in the park. You'll need to stop by the visitor center first to obtain a free permit; you can get one up to 48 hours in advance. Unfortunately, the Las Conchas Fire of 2011 burned many of the ponderosa pines and trees, meaning that subsequent monsoons flooded the canyons and washed out many trails. Check with the park staff for up-to-date information and review the Trail Condition map before venturing out. You can download several park backcountry maps on the park's website, nps.gov/band. During monsoon season (July 1–September 15), backcountry camping is closed in Frijoles, Alamo, and Capulin Canyons—the flood risk is simply too great.

The nearest town is White Rock, which has gas and other necessities. For a more detailed shopping list, you'll likely have to visit Los Alamos.

Bandelier National Monument: Juniper Family Campground

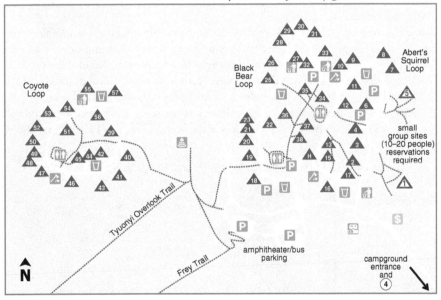

GETTING THERE

From the intersection of Rover Boulevard and NM 4 in White Rock, head west on NM 4 for about 8.5 miles. The park entrance is on your left. *Note:* The park advises that GPS may not be accurate in this area.

GPS COORDINATES: N35° 47.764' W106° 16.504'

2

⚠ Black Canyon Campground

Beauty ★★★★★ Privacy ★ Spaciousness ★ Quiet ★★★★ Security ★★★★★ Cleanliness ★★★★★

Because ponderosa pines dominate the landscape of this canyon campground, all of the sites are well shaded any time of year.

Only 8 miles from the Santa Fe plaza, this lovely little campground makes for a great week-end getaway. The scent of pine transports you from workaday worries, while the new, aesthetically appealing rockwork delights the eye. Pine, fir, maple, and oak fill the canyon, making it particularly colorful during early fall camping. The slopes of the canyon rise on either side of the campground, keeping it dark and cool late into the morning.

Black Canyon has six walk-in sites (numbered 1–6) near the entrance. Accessible by a paved walkway wide enough for wheelchairs, these tent-only sites have the most privacy and are set farther apart from one another than other sites in the campground. Site 1 sits the farthest from the rest; site 6 is the largest, but you can hear the camp host's generator from across the road. During the summer, these sites are lush, verdant spaces. Unfortunately, all of the walk-in sites are close to the highway, so there is traffic noise, particularly during the day. At night, this noise is greatly reduced.

Recently renovated, more sites are wheelchair accessible than not—a notable exception is site 29, which does not have level parking and therefore is not appropriate for RVs or trailers and likely would not be suitable for those in wheelchairs. All of the sites are level and well maintained, with clearly defined gravel tent pads. In addition to picnic tables and fire rings with attached grills, all sites also have lantern hooks for hanging your lights, trash receptacles, and the like. The charming rockwork at the sites, cabin-style vault toilets, and pay phone give Black Canyon an upscale feel. Restrooms, bear-proof trash bins, and water

The Vista Grande Overlook offers an impressive view of Santa Fe and the Sandia Mountains in the distance.

spigots are well spaced throughout the camp. When I visited, there was a problem with the electricity line to the water pump and the spigots were turned off; however, the host was hopeful the problem would be resolved and the water would be turned back on.

Channels of water cut down the canyon walls during heavy rains, but the renovation accounted for water runoff, and seasonal creeks run in rock-lined ditches along the road. Because ponderosa pines dominate the landscape of this canyon campground, all of the sites are well shaded any time of year. However, that also means the campground feels very open, and fewer spaces afford much privacy. Site 19, for instance, looks great from the road—shady, set back a little—but the picnic table nearly abuts the other sites on the inside of the loop. Site 24 lies tucked behind some thick maples and oaks, hidden from the road. Beside it, you'll find the trailhead for Black Canyon Trail 181, a 1.5-mile lollipop jaunt. Lined with thimbleberries in the late summer, this wide trail has an easy, continuous grade, making it a favorite for families. Several people who live in nearby neighborhoods regularly exercise here or come to walk their dogs. (*Note:* The trailhead parking is located outside of the campground, not at site 24.)

Even though Black Canyon is close to the city and popular with those seeking a change of pace, the campground doesn't get rowdy on the weekends. The camp host told me that loud parties tended to prefer the nearby dispersed camping or the 10 sites at nearby Big Tesuque Campground, which does not have a host. In addition to a diligent camp host, the Santa Fe County Sheriff's Department visits on a regular basis.

Santa Fe has plenty of opportunities for exploration, and there's more to do nearby. Chamisa Trail, a 4.5-mile loop, offers a steep hike through serene evergreen forest. Hyde Memorial State Park, right next to the campground, has several short trails varying in length from 0.5 mile to 2.2 miles. Many follow or cross Little Tesuque Creek, making them especially fun for children. NM 475 offers stunning views—from the Vista Grande Overlook, you can see all of the city below—and dead-ends at Ski Santa Fe. From there you can pick up several longer, more difficult trails that lead into Pecos Wilderness. After a day spent on the trails, you can stop by Ten Thousand Waves (4 miles west on NM 475 toward Santa Fe), a Japanese-themed spa, for a soak in their communal pool.

Black Canyon Campground

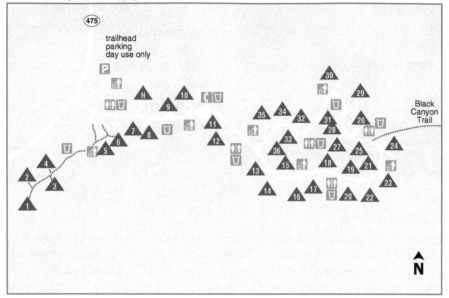

GETTING THERE

From the intersection of Bishop's Lodge Road and Artist Road in Santa Fe, head east on Artist Road, which turns into Hyde Park Road/NM 475. After about 7.5 miles, the campground will be on your right.

GPS COORDINATES: N35° 43.525' W105° 50.393'

3

⛺ Blackjack Campground

Beauty ★★★★★ Privacy ★★★ Spaciousness ★★★★★ Quiet ★★★★ Security ★★★ Cleanliness ★★★

Along Blackjack's trail, thick gooseberry bushes and tall grasses are dotted with purple from blooming asters and nodding onions.

After the town of Eagle Nest, US 64 drops into narrow Cimarron Canyon and the road begins to wind, slowing cars to 25 mph. The reduced speed gives you a chance to admire the cliffs—steep walls of crenellated granite, some of them 300 feet tall.

Blackjack Campground stretches between the road and Cimarron River, and while many sites are close to the water, none feel close to the highway. The scrub oak, Douglas-fir, and ponderosa pines obscure not only the road but also work to hide other campsites. Along the camping trail, thick gooseberry bushes and tall grasses are dotted with purple from blooming asters and nodding onions.

Each campsite has a picnic table, bear box, and campfire ring. Before you build a fire, though, check with the park rangers—the 2018 Ute Park Fire burned nearly 40,000 acres; along US 64, the standing black trees serve as a reminder to stay fire-wise. Unfortunately, the only toilet for this campground is a plastic vault toilet in the parking lot.

Each of the nine sites is spacious: when I visited, many had several tents to a site or obviously had room for campers to select the choicest spot to set up. Site 30 is the farthest down the trail, meaning it's farther to haul all of your car-camping supplies, but there's less

The Cimarron River runs through Blackjack Campground.

KEY INFORMATION

LOCATION: US 64, Eagle Nest, NM 87718

CONTACT: Cimarron Canyon State Park,
575-377-6271, emnrd.state.nm.us/SPD
/cimarroncanyonstatepark.html

OPEN: Memorial Day–Labor Day weekend

SITES: 9, all tent-only

EACH SITE HAS: Picnic table, fire ring, bear box

WHEELCHAIR ACCESS: None at this campground, but wheelchair sites are available at
Tolby and Maverick Campgrounds, which
are also part of Cimarron Canyon State Park.

ASSIGNMENT: First-come, first-served;
no reservations

REGISTRATION: On-site

AMENITIES: Vault toilet in parking lot

PARKING: Shared lot at entrance

FEE: $8/night

ELEVATION: 7,794'

RESTRICTIONS

PETS: Allowed on leashes up to 10 feet long;
don't leave pets unattended

QUIET HOURS: 10 p.m.–7 a.m.

FIRES: In fire rings only

ALCOHOL: Permitted

OTHER: Checkout at 2 p.m.; no rock climbing;
check fire restrictions

foot traffic and more privacy. It has several trees to hang a hammock or even toss a tarp up. Sites 22 and 24 would be great to grab for a group; they're close to each other and nicely wooded. Site 26 is the most open; the site is a small field between the trail and the highway, with plenty of room to spread out.

Along US 64, you'll also see Tolby, Maverick, and Ponderosa Campgrounds. All told, Cimarron Canyon State Park has 93 campsites, but Blackjack is the best spot for tent camping. From mid-May through mid-September, however, you can refill your 5-gallon jug from the other campgrounds' potable water spigots, use their plumbed and lit restrooms, and even purchase firewood from their camp hosts for $5 a bucket. The park's visitor center is at Tolby Campground.

Stocked with rainbow trout, the Cimarron River is also home to brown trout—some estimates range as high as 3,000 trout per mile. You may see deer, elk, or bears from afar, so make sure to pack your binoculars or telephoto lens. Closer encounters might include turkeys and grouse along the trails.

Just across the road from Blackjack Campground, the Jasper and Agate Trails start near mile marker 293. As you head north along the old logging road, keep your eye out for the namesake stones. Areas for anglers include Gravel Pits Lake, Perryville, Horseshoe Mine, and Tolby. From Tolby, you can also hike the 4.2-mile Tolby Meadow Trail, which joins the 3.2-mile Tolby Creek Trail to make a loop. Maverick Trail follows a creek into the canyon and splits after 0.7 mile; if you turn right, the trail continues another mile, or you can head straight to hike a little more than a mile. These trails do not connect and are out-and-back. The main canyon leads to Touch-Me-Not and Green Mountains. Additionally, you'll find the climbing hot spots at Cimarron Canyon Crags—Maverick Cliff and Probe 1 Cliff—inside the state park.

Situated in the center of the Colin Neblett Wildlife Management Area, Cimarron Canyon State Park and nearby trails have some special restrictions. Each summer from May 15 to July 31, the Tolby and Maverick Trails close to allow deer to fawn and elk to calve in peace. Clear Creek Trail, which crisscrosses the creek upstream and uphill and has several log footbridges to keep you dry, remains open during this time. Clear Creek also has many photogenic waterfalls. Only licensed deer and hunters may camp in the backcountry.

While those palisades may look tempting to climb, rock climbing is strictly prohibited anywhere within the 33,116 acres of Colin Neblett. Also, don't pick up hitchhikers—the Eagle Nest Reintegration Center is nearby. Tales of gold mining, gunslingers, and ghost towns fill the air at Eagle Nest, the closest town for services. Home to fewer than 300 people year-round, the village is a ski gateway during the winter; Angel Fire, Red River, and Taos ski resorts are also nearby. On the eastern side of the state park, Cimarron also has services and an interesting history: a land dispute here became a 15-year-long county war in the late 19th century.

Blackjack Campground

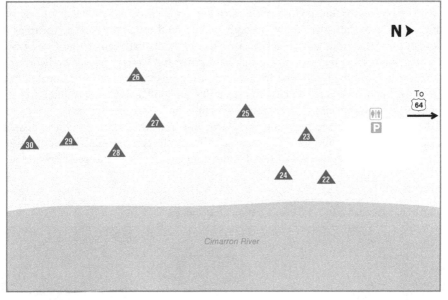

GETTING THERE

From the intersection of US 64 and NM 68 in Taos, take US 64 East toward Eagle Nest for 31 miles. About 7 miles east of Eagle Nest, you'll enter Cimarron Canyon State Park. Blackjack will be the second campground on your right.

GPS COORDINATES: N36° 31.834′ W105° 10.350′

4

⛺ Canjilon Lakes Campgrounds

Beauty ★★★ Privacy ★★★ Spaciousness ★★★★★ Quiet ★★★★ Security ★★★ Cleanliness ★★★★

To visit Canjilon Lakes Campgrounds is to witness tremendous loss—and a great regeneration effort by the U.S. Forest Service.

Canjilon Lakes Campground first opened in 1948, and 70 years later it reopened to campers and fishermen after several years of closure due to a massive tree die-off. Once covered in lush high alpine forest, this campground and the surrounding 1,000 acres of the Carson National Forest suffered substantially from drought, disease, and bugs. One silviculturist (an arborist who cares for forests) from the El Rito Ranger District blamed the deforestation on graffiti carved into the aspen. These "arborglyphs" sliced through the bark, so the trees were no longer protected from fatal fungal diseases, namely sooty bark canker and *Cytospora* canker. Then, about 15 years ago, western tent caterpillar and western spruce budworm numbers increased, and the bugs came back season after season. By 2017 an estimated 80% of the mature aspen, fir, and spruce had died. To visit Canjilon Lakes Campground is to witness tremendous loss—and a great regeneration effort by the U.S. Forest Service.

The aspens are already springing back, growing from their shared subterranean root ball. A few nice, tall firs and spruces remain standing in the campground. Many of the clearcut trees have been left as piles of wood—meaning there's abundant free firewood at this

Several small lakes, between 2 and 6 acres, attract local anglers.

KEY INFORMATION

LOCATION: FS 129, Canjilon, NM 87515

CONTACT: Carson National Forest,
Canjilon Ranger District, 575-684-2489,
tinyurl.com/canjilonlakes

OPEN: End of May–September

SITES: Lower Canjilon Lake, 11;
Middle Canjilon Lake, 31

EACH SITE HAS: Picnic table, fire ring

WHEELCHAIR ACCESS: None

ASSIGNMENT: First-come, first-served;
no reservations

REGISTRATION: On-site at kiosk

AMENITIES: Vault toilets

PARKING: At sites

FEE: $5/night ($2.50 with Interagency Pass)

ELEVATION: 9,997'

RESTRICTIONS

PETS: Permitted on leash

QUIET HOURS: 10 p.m.–6 a.m.

FIRES: In fire rings only

ALCOHOL: Permitted

OTHER: 14-day stay limit, $5/night
per extra vehicle, 22' maximum RV length

site. Wildflowers have filled the meadow. Six small lakes draw fishermen throughout the summer, although locals report that the fishing is only good in the middle and upper lakes. While this campground might score a mediocre beauty rating in 2019, in a few years it will likely charm most campers—and, with taller trees, afford greater privacy.

Canjilon Lakes has two campgrounds. The first one has 11 sites and is just across the road from Lower Canjilon Lake. Most of those who are fishing head up to the Middle Lake and camp there, or they continue on to the Upper Lake, which is the largest and has a day-use area. On either side of this quiet loop, you'll find vault toilets and bear-proof trash bins. Please note that there is no potable water at this site or the larger campground up the road.

The middle campground has three loops, each with vault toilets and trash bins. Many sites have two picnic tables. Site 20 is open on one side to the meadow, with a nice flat area for a tent, and has a good stand of aspen alongside the other half of the site. Site 21 has excellent privacy thanks to a thicket of young aspen. Site 27 has a great view of the forest; site 38 has a lovely view of the lake.

Sites 16 and 23 look like they haven't been used in a long time, and I couldn't find a fire pit at 23. Behind sites 32 and 33 there's a pond, and therefore more mosquitoes. There is evidence of cows coming through the campground, which usually means the flies are worse. In some areas, the grass is waist-high—if you have allergies, don't forget to bring your meds.

On a midsummer Friday, I had my pick of the sites. No one was camping at Lower Canjilon Lake Campground, and very few had staked out sites at the larger campground. Most people were camped along the loop with sites 35–44, which was closest to Middle Canjilon Lake. One woman pulled a 22-inch trout out of the lake; another couple offered me a bite of the trout they were cooking over a campfire.

Rangers and officers frequent the lakes, so make sure to have your fishing license handy if you're planning on catching trout. El Vado Ranch, in the town of Tierra Amarilla (32 miles northwest), sells fishing licenses and equipment. Tierra Amarilla may also be your best bet for gas and small necessities if you don't stop in Abiquiu on the way (44 miles south).

Nearby hikes are filled with scenic vistas and streams. Canjilon Mountain Trail 54 begins at the Upper Canjilon Lake picnic ground, leading you through high hills and steadily climbing drainages to Cabin Lookout. From there you can turn north, following the ridge-line into wildflower-filled meadows to the Continental Divide Trail. You may need to keep an eye out for the carsonite signs and rock cairns to stay on the trail through the meadow. You can hike the Continental Divide Trail south, following Canjilon Creek, and return to the day-use area at Upper Canjilon Lake. This is a high-altitude hike, staying between 10,000 and 11,000 feet, so be prepared for mountain weather during the 7-mile loop.

Canjilon Lower Lakes Campground

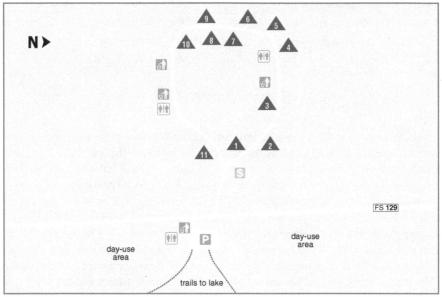

A windbreak of young aspens also provides privacy at site 20.

Canjilon Middle Lakes Campground

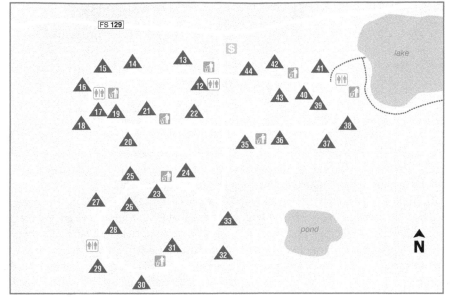

GETTING THERE

From Española, take US 84 West toward Chama. After 50 miles, turn right (east) onto NM 115 toward the town of Canjilon. Follow the signs through town to NM 110, and turn left (north). Continue for 7 miles, then turn left (north) onto Forest Service Road 129. You'll see Lower Canjilon Lake Campground on the left after 3 miles; Middle Canjilon Lake Campground is a mile farther on the right.

GPS COORDINATES: N36° 33.272' W106° 19.978'

5

♨ Chaco Culture National Historical Park: GALLO CAMPGROUND

Beauty ★★★★★ Privacy ★★ Spaciousness ★★★★ Quiet ★★★ Security ★★★★★ Cleanliness ★★★★★

The big attraction is the stunning Pueblo Bonito, one of the few American structural sites to rival Stonehenge, Teotihuacán, or Machu Picchu.

Here you can sleep at the foot of windswept ruins. Painted and pecked onto boulders lining the campground are ancient depictions of bears, pronghorn antelope, and celestial events. You'll want to leave the rainfly off your tent because the sky stretches wide above: millions of stars, the Milky Way, and the occasional satellite shine down. You could spend weeks here hiking and checking out ruins by day and stargazing all night.

Thousands of people lived or visited here between 850 and 1250 C.E. These ancient Chacoans constructed impressive buildings, many of which are aligned to solar, lunar, and cardinal directions. The monumental architecture and unique masonry here tell a story of a ceremonial, governmental, and economic hub in the San Juan Basin.

Several trails in the park lead to different ruins. These hikes are easy, but some require backcountry permits, which can be filled out at the trailheads. The big attraction is the stunning Pueblo Bonito, one of the few American structural sites to rival Stonehenge, Teotihuacán, or Machu Picchu. Built sometime between 828 and 1126 C.E., Pueblo Bonito boasts some 800 rooms, more than 30 kivas, and a central plaza, all covering 3 acres. One archaeologist has estimated that building the main structure would have taken 805,000 person-hours.

Between Kin Kletso and Peñasco Blanco, a side trail leads to a remarkable array of petroglyphs. Crossing the Chaco Wash on this same trail, you can see pictographs of the Crab

An impressive tableau of petroglyphs tells a story at the campfire circle.

KEY INFORMATION

LOCATION: 1808 CR 7950, Nageezi, NM 87037

CONTACT: Chaco Culture National Historical Park, 505-786-7014, nps.gpv/chcu

OPEN: Year-round, but note that the park is closed on Thanksgiving Day, Christmas Day, and New Year's Day.

SITES: 38, including 2 group sites

EACH SITE HAS: Parking space, picnic table, fire ring with grill, tent pads; 2 hiking trails start at campground; cliff dwellings and petroglyphs accessible from campsites

WHEELCHAIR ACCESS: Site 11 and restrooms

ASSIGNMENT: First-come, first-served (8 sites) and by reservation (877-444-6777, recreation .gov/camping/campgrounds/250009)

REGISTRATION: At visitor center

AMENITIES: 2 bathhouses with dump sinks and running, nonpotable water; 2 water spigots at visitor center

PARKING: At sites

FEE: $15/night individual sites ($7.50 with Interagency Pass), $60/night group sites. Park-entrance fee is $25/vehicle for 7 days.

ELEVATION: 6,200'

RESTRICTIONS

PETS: Allowed on leashes in the backcountry but not within archaeological sites

QUIET HOURS: 8 p.m.–8 a.m.

FIRES: In fire rings only; gathering firewood is prohibited. Check with park staff or camp hosts for up-to-date fire restrictions.

ALCOHOL: Permitted at sites only

OTHER: 14-day stay limit; generators may be operated 1 hour at a time between 8 a.m. and 8 p.m.

Nebula supernova, which became "a guest star" that shone day and night for 23 days in 1054 C.E. Just below it, the Chacoans also recorded Halley's Comet.

All trails close at sunset and reopen at 7 a.m. Chaco Culture is ancestral land for many Pueblo peoples of the Southwest, so please respect this sacred land and the delicate, irreplaceable archaeology here. Stay on designated trails and leave artifacts in place, even the pottery sherds you may find in the campground.

The park hosts tours of the various structures, along with evening campfire talks and night-sky interpretive programs. Chaco Culture is an International Dark Sky Park, recognized as one of America's best stargazing sites—there is no permanent outdoor lighting in 99% of the park. The visitor center has an observatory and telescopes that visitors can use during night-sky programs.

Gallo Campground sits a mile down the road from the visitor center. From the campground, there are two easy hiking trails: the Fajada Butte Overlook takes you up and across a mesa, and the Wijiji Trail leads to a symmetrical structure from the 1100s and more rock art.

Bats and swallows glide from the cliffs at night. Ravens have been known to open backpacks left at camp and tear open packages, looking for something to eat. Nuthatches and canyon towhees will also visit campsites, perching on shrubs and begging for handouts—don't fall for their cute antics.

In the late spring, blooming cactus, globemallow, asters, and many more wildflowers brighten the desert valley. Saltbrush, wolfberry, and cliff rose dot campsites. There are few trees and little relief from the sun; if you have room in your car for a shade structure, bring it. Heatstroke is one of the common problems visitors experience (see page 11 for more information). The tent pads have rings to tie down tents in the event of strong winds, which are common. Summers are hot, and sudden, violent thunderstorms can occur during monsoon season. Over the course of one day, temperatures can fluctuate over 60 degrees, so it's best to be prepared for varying weather conditions.

During the extended closure brought on by the pandemic, the park reconfigured the campground and decided to close the former tent-only camping loop that hugged the cliffs. They feared that some of the cliff was growing unstable and could pose a hazard to camping. However, you can still walk among the fallen boulders and view petroglyphs, including an impressive bear-footprint petroglyph. Ancient cliff houses and petroglyphs lie behind sites 21–27, viewable by a short trail running behind the sites to the campfire circle.

Two restrooms with flush toilets; running, nonpotable water; and dump sinks are in the campground. Closed from the day after Veterans Day until the end of February, these bathrooms are replaced with portable toilets. There are two recycling bins and trash cans. The campground does not have potable water, but you can fill water containers at the visitor center, which has two spigots available 24 hours a day. There are no services—no gas or auto repair, no food—inside the park. The nearest convenience store is 21 miles from the campground, so come prepared with ice, sunblock, and other necessities.

Chaco Culture National Historical Park: Gallo Campground

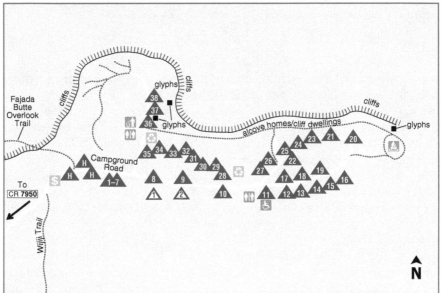

GETTING THERE

From Albuquerque, drive north on US 550 about 130 miles; then, about 50 miles past the town of Cuba, turn left (south) onto County Road 7900. In 5.1 miles, turn right (southwest) onto CR 7950. In 7.6 miles, bear left (south) to stay on CR 7950, and in another 4.2 miles, turn left again (south) to continue on this road. In 0.6 mile turn left (south) onto an unnamed road, and in 0.3 mile turn left again (southeast) onto CR 7950. In 4.4 miles, turn right (north) onto Campground Road. The campground entrance is about 0.3 mile ahead. From US 550 to the park boundary, the route—marked with brown National Park Service signage—includes about 13 miles of rough dirt road and 4.5 miles of very rough washboard. Use caution crossing the wash when any water is present.

From Farmington, head south on US 550, and in about 52 miles, turn right onto CR 7900. Then follow the directions above, starting with the second sentence.

Another entrance to the south is accessible from east- or westbound I-40 (Exit 53) in Thoreau—right (north) onto NM 371, right (east) onto NM 57, and then left (north) to stay on NM 57, a distance of about 60 miles—on a much more rugged road. Call the park for up-to-date road conditions before attempting this entrance. *Note:* Visitors have reported that GPS devices may not be accurate in the Chaco area.

GPS COORDINATES: N36° 02.161' W107° 53.482'

The ruins at Chaco Canyon display intricate brickwork worthy of closer inspection.

6

⛺ Clear Creek Campground

Beauty ★★★★★ Privacy ★★★★ Spaciousness ★★★★★ Quiet ★★★★ Security ★★★★★ Cleanliness ★★★★★

Aerobatic mountain chickadees and bold Steller's jays are also drawn to Clear Creek Campground—probably for some of the same reasons many New Mexicans come to camp here summer after summer.

While setting up your tent between the tall ponderosas, you may hear the whispering trills, watch-winding sounds, and upsweeping high notes of the pine siskin. Aerobatic mountain chickadees and bold Steller's jays are also drawn to Clear Creek Campground—probably for some of the same reasons many New Mexicans come to camp here summer after summer. At over 8,000 feet in elevation, the air is fresh and cool, as well as scented with a relaxing aroma of pine. Clear Creek runs along the back side of the lower-numbered campsites, filling the air with the tranquil babble of water flowing over smooth stones. Only 2 hours from Albuquerque and less crowded than the popular Jemez Mountains campgrounds near Jemez Springs, Clear Creek Campground makes for a great weekend getaway in the summer and fall.

The 12 campsites are all laid along a central road in a meadow, with pull-offs for parking directly at your chosen site. From the entrance, the first site on the right is the camp host's space. In the main campground, there are two vault toilets (near sites 2 and 5) and one water spigot (near site 4). While officially there is only one ADA site, both campsites 1 and

In addition to trout, you might spot salamanders and skinks near the cool water of Clear Creek.

KEY INFORMATION

LOCATION: NM 126, 11 miles east of Cuba

CONTACT: Santa Fe National Forest,
Cuba Ranger District; 575-289-3264,
tinyurl.com/clearcreekcampground

OPEN: May 15–September 30

SITES: 12, plus 1 group site

EACH SITE HAS: Picnic table, fire ring

WHEELCHAIR ACCESS: 1 accessible site
plus accessible toilets

ASSIGNMENT: First-come, first-served only
September 15–30; otherwise reserve online
(877-447-6777, recreation.gov/camping
/campgrounds/251358)

REGISTRATION: Online in season
(on-site September 15–30)

AMENITIES: Vault toilets, potable water

PARKING: At sites

FEE: $10/night ($5 with Interagency Pass),
$35/night group site

ELEVATION: 8,350'

RESTRICTIONS

PETS: Allowed on leashes

QUIET HOURS: 10 p.m.–6 a.m.

FIRES: In fire rings only

ALCOHOL: Permitted at sites

OTHER: ATVs prohibited; $10/additional vehicle;
maximum 8 people/site. Trailers are limited to
16' in length; RVs, 30'. Do not collect artifacts.
Cell reception is poor here.

2 appear accessible; wholly paved around the fire ring and picnic table, they have space to set up a tent on the asphalt RV pad. Site 2 also has a paved walkway leading to site 3. Site 4 seems particularly nice: it has quite a few evergreens surrounding it and sits a little farther from the other campsites. Sites 5, 6, and 7 are a little clustered and would be great to reserve with friends and family. If you venture too far from the fire ring to pitch your tent, watch out for mole tunnels.

At the top of the loop, you'll find the group site behind a gate. This area costs $35/night, hosts up to 35 people overnight, and is reservable online. The group area has its own toilet facilities, a pedestal grill, and a large shelter with half a dozen picnic tables. In addition to three tent pads, there are spaces for two RVs.

This campground—along with nearby Rio de las Vacas (see page 73)—is popular with anglers. Rio Grande cutthroat trout are native to the waters; you might also catch rainbow and brown trout. Even if you aren't fishing, you can still enjoy Clear Creek, especially with children eager to play in the cold water. Keep an eye out for tiger salamanders and five-lined skinks near the banks. While exploring the general vicinity of the campground and nearby forest, you may stumble on ruins or other archaeological artifacts. Remember to leave these items where you find them, and do not disturb sites.

Across from the campground's entrance on NM 126, there is a day-use picnic area with additional tables and grills, as well as access to the forest. Both the picnic area and the campground have cattle guards to keep the cows grazing outside. When I visited, however, the cows had apparently found a way into the campground—several cow pies were left as evidence. Watch for them along the highway, as cows sometimes graze near the road.

The nearby San Pedro Parks Wilderness has more than 41,000 acres of forest to enjoy. Named for the meadows, or "parks," that pepper the alpine forest, San Pedro Parks includes the Nacimiento Mountains, a western finger of the Rocky Mountains. In the parks, Rocky Mountain iris blooms purple next to bluegrass, and you may see elk, deer, or wild turkeys. The Continental Divide Trail cuts through here, following the Los Pinos, Vacas, Penas Negras, and

Rio Capulin Trails. The most popular hike is Vacas Trail, a roughly 10-mile trek through Engelmann spruce to San Pedro Park. It's a steady climb with minimal grade and several streams for fresh water, making it a good trail for beginner backpackers. From the same trailhead, you can also opt to hike a mile to San Gregorio Lake, a small reservoir. Note that motorized and mechanized use is prohibited in this wilderness—that is, no ATVs or bikes.

Cuba, only 11 miles away, will have most of what you need in the form of extra groceries and gas. For a town small enough not to warrant a stoplight, it has several great restaurants.

Clear Creek Campground

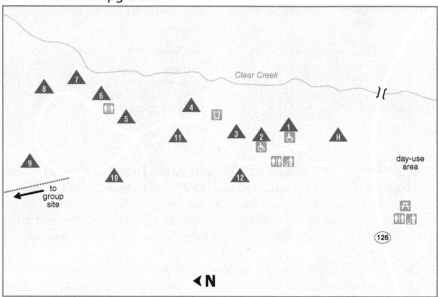

GETTING THERE

From US 550 in Cuba, turn east onto NM 126 at the visitor information center. After 11.4 miles, the campground will be on your left (north).

GPS COORDINATES: N35° 59.783′ W106° 49.598′

7

⛺ Cochiti Lake and Tetilla Peak Campgrounds

Beauty ★★★ Privacy ★★ Spaciousness ★★ Quiet ★★ Security ★★★★ Cleanliness ★★★★

In addition to flood control, this no-wake lake provides plenty of opportunity to swim, kayak, paddleboard, canoe, water-ski, sail, and fish.

During the long, hot days of summer, do you dream of leaping into a cool lake? Such a place seems improbable so close to Albuquerque, but in 1975, with the completion of a 5.3-mile-long dam, Cochiti Lake was formed. This earthen dam is one of the 10 longest in the world. Working in conjunction with three other dams—Abiquiu, Galisteo, and Jemez Canyon Dams—the Cochiti Dam keeps the Rio Grande from flooding Albuquerque. In addition to flood control, this no-wake lake provides plenty of opportunity to swim, kayak, paddleboard, canoe, water-ski, sail, and fish.

After an afternoon spent swimming, you can walk back to your campsite at Cochiti Lake.

KEY INFORMATION

LOCATION: 82 Dam Crest Road, Peña Blanca, NM 87041-5015

CONTACT: U.S. Army Corps of Engineers, 505-465-0307, tinyurl.com/cochitilake

OPEN: Cochiti Lake, year-round; Tetilla Peak, April–October

SITES: Cochiti Lake, 129; Tetilla Peak, 54

EACH SITE HAS: Picnic table, pedestal grill; many have shade structures and lantern hooks

WHEELCHAIR ACCESS: None

ASSIGNMENT: First-come, first-served only mid-October–November 30 and March 1–mid-April; otherwise reserve online (877-444-6777, recreation.gov/camping /campgrounds/233461, recreation.gov /camping/campgrounds/233649)

REGISTRATION: Self-register on-site or online

AMENITIES: Boat ramp, swimming area, visitor center, showers, flush toilets, water, RV hookups, dump station

PARKING: At sites

FEE: $12/night nonelectric sites, $20/night electric sites

ELEVATION: 5,343'

RESTRICTIONS

PETS: Allowed on leash

QUIET HOURS: 10 p.m.–6 a.m.

FIRES: Prohibited; only charcoal allowed in grills

ALCOHOL: Not permitted

OTHER: 14-day stay limit; checkout at 2 p.m.; life vests required for any water activity other than swimming

Cochiti Lake Campground is the main campground, on the west side of the lake, and Tetilla Peak Campground sits above the eastern edge, overlooking the river. Each has a boat ramp and water access.

In the summer of 2019, long, warm days and still water created the right conditions for a toxic algae bloom in the lake. Because blue-green algae (cyanobacteria) can cause health problems if ingested, inhaled, or even touched, the U.S. Army Corps of Engineers closed the lake to swimming and advised caution during all other water recreation. Fish—the lake is home to channel catfish, largemouth bass, northern pike, walleye, and white crappie—could still be eaten in moderation. Check tinyurl.com/cochitilake for the latest information about closures.

Made up of four loops plus a group camping area and a day-use loop, Cochiti Lake Campground offers plenty of sites to choose from. Each loop has nearby bathroom and shower facilities. Set the farthest from the lake, the Juniper Loop has electric hookups and most sites have water; together with Buffalo Grove Loop, Juniper Loop is intended for RV camping. Elk Run Loop and Ringtail Cat Loop aren't designated as tent-specific, but they don't offer electricity and they have only three water spigots apiece, so they are less frequented by RVs.

Ringtail Cat Loop seems the best for tent campers—sites 67–73 all overlook the lake. Each site has a shade structure, lantern pole, picnic table, pedestal grill, and tent pad. In particular, sites 67 and 69 look nice; in addition to a good view, they have rows of junipers for extra privacy, shade, and windbreak.

Tetilla Peak Campground, on the opposite shore, provides views of the Rio Grande and the lake. RVers can choose from 54 sites in two loops; the tent-specific area has 10 sites. In addition to three restrooms (no showers), there are five water spigots. Far enough away from the main entry for recreation, Tetilla Peak has a quieter setting, with no homes or buildings in view.

None of the sites in either campground have rings for campfires. You can understand why fires aren't permitted at this campground—when I visited in mid-September, it was hot, hot, hot and the grasses surrounding the sites had turned crispy. There are few trees—some junipers and Apache plumes are your best chance for shade other than a permanent shade structure. If you plan to spend time on the lake and retire to the campground afterward, make sure to bring sunblock and perhaps a parasol.

Cochiti Lake is the only campground where I've seen a rattlesnake: a thick western diamondback, coiled under a shrubby juniper, shook its tiny maraca when we met. Do watch where you step, and if you hear that characteristic rattle, give it a large amount of personal space.

You can hike the Nashroo! Trail system, which leads from the visitor center to the swimming beach, boat launch, and Dam Crest Road. The Cochiti people speak the Keres language, and *Nashroo!* is a Keres word meaning "Let's go!" Today, 1,175 Pueblo members live on the 84 square miles of reservation that includes the dam and lake; please be considerate of their land. Some parcels of land are off-limits to visitors; these are posted. You can learn more about Cochiti Pueblo at the visitor center at the NM 22 junction.

Right outside of Cochiti Pueblo is Kasha-Katuwe Tent Rocks, a beautiful national monument with incredible geologic features. Winding slot canyons and cone-shaped hoodoos will delight photographers and explorers alike. If you choose to summit the plateau, you'll not only have an astonishing view of the surrounding desert but also be able to see down onto the tent-shaped formations. *Note:* Dogs are not allowed in the monument.

Cochiti Lake Campground

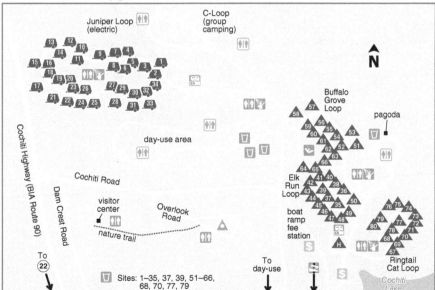

Cochiti Lake: Tetilla Peak Campground

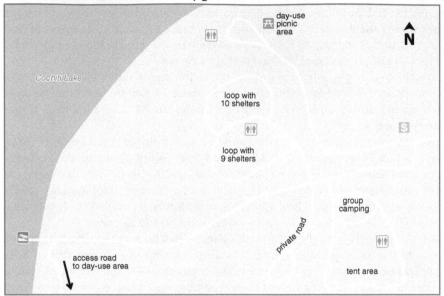

GETTING THERE

From the intersection of I-25 and I-40 in Albuquerque, take I-25 North for 32.7 miles to Exit 259, and turn left (north) onto NM 22. Follow the signs for Cochiti Lake about 20 miles through Peña Blanca to the visitor center and campground office.

To get to Tetilla Peak, go 5.5 miles farther on I-25 to Exit 264, and turn left (west) onto NM 16; in 3.8 miles, turn right (northeast) onto Tetilla Peak Road at the sign. In about 10 miles, turn left to reach the campground entrance.

GPS COORDINATES:
    Cochiti Lake N35° 38.542′ W106° 19.429′
    Tetilla Peak N35° 38.734′ W106° 18.295′

8

Columbine Campground

Beauty ★★★★ Privacy ★★ Spaciousness ★★ Quiet ★★★ Security ★★★★★ Cleanliness ★★★★★

Bighorn sheep occasionally visit this campground.

Across the road from Columbine Campground, you'll see a molybdenum mine, which is in a shutdown process that will take decades to finish as mineshafts are backfilled and water is reclaimed and treated. (Molybdenum is used to create high-strength, lightweight alloys, such as the ones that make mountain bikes and wheelchairs lighter, faster, and more durable.) Pollution from this mine once turned Questa's teenagers' hair white and created white stripes on their fingernails—both signs of metal contamination. In the 1980s, acid drainage turned the Red River cloudy and blue. A related EPA cleanup of nearby Eagle Rock Lake has led to several improvements, including new soil in the lakebed and a paved path around the lake with fishing access. Once inside the campground, however, dense pine, spruce, and deciduous trees obscure the view of the mine's stripped ridge.

Columbine Creek cuts through part of this campground, making it a lush, riparian camping experience. The creek connects with Red River near the road. The campground has several pretty spots to pitch your tent along the creek, surrounded by tall grass, wildflowers, and trees. You can fish in Columbine Creek with artificial flies or a single, barbless hook. The "Red Chile Water" designation of the creek means a catch-and-release restriction

A local outfitter prepares a pack llama adventure at Columbine Campground.

KEY INFORMATION

LOCATION: 184 NM 38, Red River, NM 87558

CONTACT: Carson National Forest, Questa Ranger District, 575-586-0520, tinyurl.com /columbinecampground; Scenic Canyons (concessionaire), 435-245-6521, sceniccanyons.com

OPEN: Mid-May–Mid-September

SITES: 27

EACH SITE HAS: Picnic table, fire ring with grill

WHEELCHAIR ACCESS: Sites 1 and 8

ASSIGNMENT: First-come, first-served and by reservation (877-444-6777, recreation.gov /camping/campgrounds/251436)

REGISTRATION: Online or on-site

AMENITIES: Vault toilets, potable water from pumps

PARKING: At sites

FEE: $18/night ($9 with Interagency Pass); $5/additional vehicle

ELEVATION: 7,986'

RESTRICTIONS

PETS: Allowed on leash

QUIET HOURS: 10 p.m.–6 a.m.

FIRES: In fire rings only

ALCOHOL: Prohibited

OTHER: 14-day stay limit; 8 people/campsite; check-in at noon, checkout at 2 p.m. No ATVs or horses driven through camp. Do not clean fish in water spigots. Firewood for sale with camp host. Access to Columbine-Twining National Recreation Trail from campground.

for Rio Grande cutthroat trout, but there's no bag limit for rainbow trout, brown trout, and brook trout. *Note:* The Red River has a bag limit of five fish per day.

Due to the layout, sites 1, 2, 9, 10, and 11 all feel very crowded. Sites 1–8 have concrete pads but offer easy access to the river. Sites 1 and 8 are accessible and conveniently situated by a vault toilet. Site 16 seems small at first glance but has a nicely hidden, level spot to erect a tent down by the creek. Nestled in a stand of trees by the creek, sites 26 and 27 offer the best seclusion; these two are walk-up only and cannot be reserved online. Sites 15, 17, and 18 are nice alternatives if you prefer a reservation. Four vault toilets are spread throughout the campground, as well as pumps with potable water. This campground, like the others along NM 38, doesn't have electricity.

The camp host warned me that on NM 38 there are frequent accidents with wildlife, particularly mule deer, bighorn sheep, and elk, so take caution while driving between Questa and Red River, especially at night. Bighorn sheep occasionally come into the campsite. Bears and bobcats also frequent this area, so keep your pets leashed and children in sight. You'll see plenty of chipmunks and hummingbirds here too—some campers even put out hummingbird feeders, but lock those away at night to keep black bears from stopping by your tent to guzzle the simple syrup.

You might also see packhorses and pack llamas staging for trips between sites 18 and 19, where there's a parking lot and access to the Columbine-Twining National Recreation Trail. Columbine Canyon Trail 71, as well as the Cold Hill, Lobo Peak, and Twining Trails, starts at this trailhead south of the campground. The trail crisscrosses Columbine Creek, following a route used by gold miners and prospectors during the mining boom of the late 1800s.

If this campground is full, you may be able to find a spot at Goat Hill Campground, which is maintained by the same camp host. Goat Hill is small—there are only six sites, all of which are first-come, first-served. There is one vault toilet and no water. Each site has a picnic table and fire ring with a grill. Snugly fit between the road and the river, Goat Hill sites are small and racked with road noise throughout the night. The nearby Bobita Campground is currently closed—the bathroom vaults collapsed, and there's no water—but opens on overflow weekends, particularly Memorial Day, when the Red River Motorcycle Rally brings in 20,000-plus bikers. The concessionaire has a relationship with Red River RV Park, which permits campers to use its coin-operated laundry and showers. You can also purchase ice there, or you can continue into town for more goods and services. Outfitters in town will take you panning for gold flakes and nuggets; Old West bank robbery reenactments start on summer weekend afternoons at 4:30 p.m. and end in time for happy hour at the local brewery or a saloon.

Columbine Campground

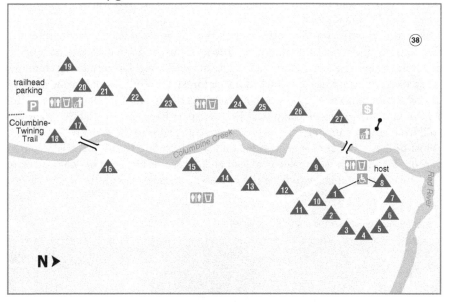

GETTING THERE

From Taos, drive north on NM 522 for 25 miles until you reach Questa. Turn right on NM 38 and drive east for 5 miles. The campground will be on the right.

GPS COORDINATES: N36° 40.644' W105° 30.941'

9

⛺ Coyote Creek State Park Campground

Beauty ★★★ Privacy ★★★ Spaciousness ★★★★ Quiet ★★★★ Security ★★★★★ Cleanliness ★★★★★

Coyote Creek State Park lies in the middle of a panorama of lush, green pine forest rolling in to the deep blue of distant mountains.

Flowing south through Guadalupita Canyon, Coyote Creek cuts across this state park before it eventually connects to the Mora River. To the east of the park, La Mesa ridge rises to 9,112 feet; to the west, you can see the Rincon subrange of the Sangre de Cristo Mountains. Coyote Creek State Park lies in the middle of a panorama of lush green pine forest rolling in to the deep blue of distant mountains—one of the few places in New Mexico where you truly see the tail end of the Rockies.

Don't dismay when you first drive in and see the rows of RVs by the bathhouse and ranger station—the rest of the campground is spacious, and the tent-specific loop seems to be set in an alternate world entirely. The Encino, or E Loop, has recently been renovated to make nice tent-camping sites. Tucked into a forested hillside, these five sites each have plenty of privacy and a woodsy feel. Ponderosa pines tower over Gambel oaks. Each site has a picnic table and fire ring for campfires. The state park has constructed brick walls to keep the hill from eroding into the campsites; this terracing adds to the privacy.

Most of these sites are big enough for only one tent. Site E4, however, is a double site with room for a few tents. Situated at a dead end, E4 seems ideal. Set back a ways from the rest of the campground, overlooking the creek and meadows, with the sound of rushing

Monsoon clouds roll in over the scenic Mora Valley.

KEY INFORMATION

LOCATION: NM 434, Mile Marker 17, Guadalupita, NM 87722

CONTACT: Coyote Creek State Park, 575-387-2328, emnrd.state.nm.us/SPD /coyotecreeklakestatepark.html

OPEN: Mid-May–Mid-September; contact park staff about walk-in camping during winter

SITES: 35

EACH SITE HAS: Picnic table, fire ring; some have Adirondack shelters

WHEELCHAIR ACCESS: Sites 17 and 20

ASSIGNMENT: First-come, first-served and by reservation (877-664-7787, newmexicostateparks.reserveamerica.com)

REGISTRATION: Self-register on-site or online

AMENITIES: Showers, potable water, bathrooms with flush toilets and sinks with running water, RV dump station; many electric sites for RVs, playground

PARKING: At sites

FEE: $8/vehicle at primitive sites, $10–$14 at developed sites

ELEVATION: 7,706'

RESTRICTIONS

PETS: Permitted on leash

QUIET HOURS: 10 p.m.–7 a.m.

FIRES: In fire rings only

ALCOHOL: Permitted at sites; no glass containers

OTHER: Reserved sites must be occupied by 4 p.m.; park closes to day-use visitors at 9 p.m.; checkout is 2 p.m.

water to lull you to sleep and its own trail leading to the water—what more could you ask for at a campground? This site even has its own bear boxes to store your food in.

If you prefer an Adirondack shelter in the meadow below, you'll find it spotless. The rangers power-wash these structures after each party packs up; they also power-wash the vault toilets daily. At the entrance of the campground, the ranger station has an adjoining set of bathrooms, complete with flush toilets, sinks with running water, showers, and a water fountain. If anything happens to the electricity, though, the water is shut off (and, of course, the RVs begin running generators). Farther down the loop, children swing and slide on a new playground structure in the middle of a meadow.

In a clearing of Gambel oak, the Youth Conservation Corps group site has its own gated road, making it a completely private campsite. The overflow primitive area is reminiscent of music-festival camping—it's little more than a large, mowed field where you can squeeze in if you're in a pinch. Don't expect the rowdy fervor of a festival, though, as the constant presence of the rangers and the diligent camp host keep the campground family-friendly, quiet, and secure.

Along the creek banks, coyote willow grows thickly—if you look, you may catch a glimpse of the endangered willow flycatcher. You'll see this southwestern subspecies of flycatcher flitting from the willows to narrowleaf cottonwood and chokecherries, perhaps calling out "whit, whit" before diving for an insect. Farther from the banks, the understory of Gambel oak, lacking any of the taller ponderosa pines, gives the impression of a short forest that children might love to play in.

The park rangers mow the meadows around the campground, but in unmaintained areas you'll likely see geraniums, sunflowers, irises, and primroses. Porcupines are known to live here, making another great reason to keep your dog appropriately leashed. If you follow the creek, you'll encounter beaver dams in several locations; the adjacent small pools may be home to rainbow trout, brown trout, Rio Grande cutthroat trout, and white suckers.

The campground has a nice little trail, about a mile long, that encircles the campground and crosses the creek twice. It's named after Eusebio Romero, a rancher who owned the land in the 1930s; from the trail, you can even see his old moonshine shack. The park plans to add a second hiking trail.

The park host sells wood for campfires. Coyote Creek is 17 miles north of Mora and about 17 miles south of Angel Fire if you need to restock on anything else. Mora has a great farmer's market; from August through October, you might also opt to pick your own raspberries at Salman Raspberry Ranch and Country Store in nearby La Cueva. The Mora National Fish Hatchery specializes in restoring the threatened Gila trout to New Mexico's high-desert watersheds. Visitors are welcome Monday–Friday, 7 a.m.–3 p.m., and Saturday, 9 a.m.–3:30 p.m.

Coyote Creek State Park Campground

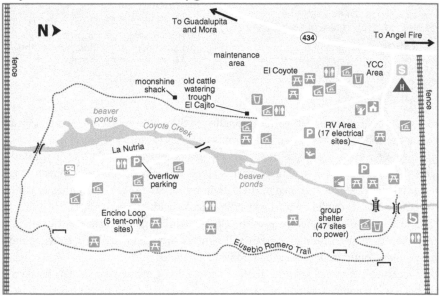

GETTING THERE

From Las Vegas, take NM 518 North toward Mora. After 25 miles, turn right (north) onto NM 434 North in Mora—this turn, by the old mill, is nearly hidden; take it slow through town so you don't miss it. After 17 miles, Coyote Creek will be on your right.

GPS COORDINATES: N36° 10.673' W105° 14.017'

10

Elephant Rock Campground

Beauty ★★★★ Privacy ★★★ Spaciousness ★★★★★ Quiet ★★★ Security ★★★★★ Cleanliness ★★★★★

Elephant Rock offers secluded camping in alpine mining country.

The people of Taos Pueblo called the river *Pee Ho Ghay Po* ("Red River Creek") because sediment stains the creek's water red. This river flows down the north slope of Mount Wheeler in the Sangre del Cristo Mountains, through the township of Red River and then through the town of Questa, and finally enters the Rio Grande south of La Junta Campground at Wild Rivers. Winter fishing here creates the unique opportunity for people visiting Taos to ski and fish during the same trip.

Elephant Rock has a particular beauty, showing a different ecosystem than the one just across the road at Red River. The ground is rocky and covered with pine needles, and the campsites are terraced into the hillside. Tall ponderosa pines and a mix of aspen, blue and silver spruce, and fir provides ample shade. Whereas Columbine, Fawn Lakes, and Junebug Campgrounds were full when I visited, Elephant Rock had several available spaces.

This campground is not as popular as those sitting right on Red River, even though there's still fishing access just across the highway and Fawn Lakes is only a half-mile walk away. The single-loop campground is on a hill; stony terraces create many of the campsites. A ravine cuts between sites 7 and 8, but the sites themselves have constructed, leveled spaces for tents. Rain doesn't appear to pool at these sites, instead flowing downhill and down the ravine. While the sites themselves have only enough leveled space for one or two

A terraced campsite at Elephant Rock

KEY INFORMATION

LOCATION: NM 38, 12 miles east of Questa and 3 miles west of Red River

CONTACT: Carson National Forest, Questa Ranger District, 575-586-0520, tinyurl.com/columbinecampground; Scenic Canyons (concessionaire), 435-245-6521, sceniccanyons.com

OPEN: Mid-May–mid-September

SITES: 21

EACH SITE HAS: Picnic table, fire ring with grill (sites 17 and 19 have pedestal grills)

WHEELCHAIR ACCESS: Sites 17 and 19; accessible toilet

ASSIGNMENT: First-come, first-served and by reservation (877-444-6777, recreation.gov /camping/campgrounds/251359)

REGISTRATION: On-site or online

AMENITIES: Vault toilets, potable water from pumps

PARKING: At sites

FEE: $18/night ($9/night with Interagency Pass); $5/additional vehicle

ELEVATION: 8,498'

RESTRICTIONS

PETS: Allowed on leash

QUIET HOURS: 10 p.m.–6 a.m.

FIRES: In fire rings only

ALCOHOL: No restrictions

OTHER: 14-day stay limit; maximum 8 people/site; no ATVs driven through camp. Firewood for sale with camp host. Do not move boundary rocks or poles.

tents maximum, the space between sites is much greater than at the other campgrounds along NM 38, providing greater privacy. Sites 2, 11, and 12 are nice for tents; 11 has a good set of trees to hang a hammock; and 12 features a lovely stand of aspen.

Sites 17 and 19 are accessible and include pedestal grills; 17 also has a ramp from the road. You can reserve sites 1–13 online, while sites 14–21 (excluding site 20, which is the host) are first-come, first-served.

There are three vault toilets (between sites 1 and 2, 6 and 7, and 16 and 17) and four water spigots throughout the camp. The water here is reclaimed and has a unique flavor that some describe as peppery.

Elephant Rock's elevation means cooler temperatures. The average summer daytime high is 75°F; the average nighttime low is 38°F. The camp host sells firewood for $6 a bundle. Carson Forest regularly has fire restrictions until monsoon season starts in July; it's worth it to check with the Questa Ranger District when planning your trip.

The concessionaire has a relationship with Red River RV Park, which permits campers to use its coin-operated laundry and showers. There you can also purchase ice, or you can continue into town for more goods and services. In town you can find outfitters for almost every adventure: ATV rentals, horse rides, llama tours, and even day trips panning for gold. Red River Brewery opened in 2018 and is one of the hot local spots. You can even ride the miner's transit shuttles to get into town and back to camp. Sprightly Abert's squirrels bound through the campground; nuthatches dance up and down the pines. Chipmunks may offer to help you keep a clean camp, but it's best not to share human food with them. Scan the rock faces for bighorn sheep. Nearer to the river, you're likely to see a lovely bouquet of wildflowers, including aster, cinquefoil, columbine, daisy, fairy trumpet, fireweed, mariposa lily, mountain iris, penstemon, and scarlet paintbrush.

To see the Elephant Rock formation, travel west on NM 38 for about 0.5 mile, pull off on the south side of the road, and look directly north up the wash. While Elephant Rock has a trail, it's intended use is for motorcyclists and wouldn't make for good hiking. Luckily, there are several great hiking trails in the area, including the Columbine-Twining National Recreation Trail accessible at the Columbine Campground (see page 37); Middle Fork Lake Trail, Lost Lake Trail, and Horseshoe Lake Trail, accessible from Forest Service Road 58; and, of course, Wheeler Peak Trail, which leads you up the summit of the highest peak in New Mexico and can be accessed either from Middle Fork Lake (the shorter route, 7 miles one way) or Horseshoe Lake (10 miles one-way).

From late May through November, many hikers may use the campgrounds along NM 38 for an initial rest before summiting Mount Wheeler, New Mexico's highest peak. Two main routes to the top offer a rewarding mountaineering experience. The Bull-of-the-Woods Trail follows a well-marked trail for the duration of the 16-mile round-trip hike. Williams Lake Trail, on the other hand, is only 8 miles out-and-back, but it's steep and the final 1,000-foot climb is a rocky, scree slope. Most of the hikes are at elevations between 8,000 and 10,000 feet, and Wheeler Peak lies at 13,161 feet, so if you plan to hike, take plenty of water.

There's more camping at Junebug Campground (not profiled in this edition) across the highway. At Junebug you can pitch your tent right along the banks of the icy Red River and fish at your campsite—or use it as a base for the many recreation opportunities available in the valley.

Elephant Rock Campground

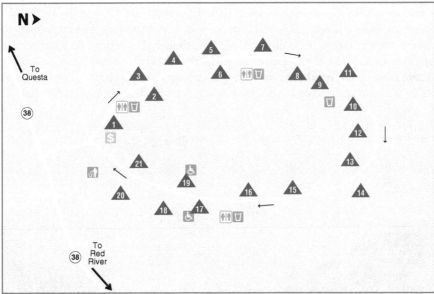

GETTING THERE

From Taos, drive north on NM 522 for 25 miles until you reach Questa. Then turn right on NM 38 and drive east for 9 miles. The campsite will be on the left.

GPS COORDINATES: N36° 42.360' W105° 27.392'

11

⚠ Fawn Lakes Campground

Beauty ★★★★ Privacy ★★ Spaciousness ★★★ Quiet ★★★ Security ★★★★★ Cleanliness ★★★★★

You can see the fish jumping from the green water in the middle of the lakes even at high noon.

Named for two man-made ponds, Fawn Lakes makes for a fun site for a family weekend of camping and fishing. Red River runs adjacent to the lakes, which are surrounded by cattails, thistles, and tall asters. You can see the fish jumping from the green water in the middle of the lakes even at high noon. A day-use parking lot outside of the campground fills up quickly in the summer and provides access for ice fishing in the winter. In Fawn Lakes and the nearby river, you can catch brook, brown, cutthroat, German, and rainbow trout—salmon and pike might also nibble on your fly. If you happen to catch a Rio Grande trout, gently release it back into the river. In addition to fishing, the lakes have nice walkways that make popular strolls, particularly for older campers and children. Kids also love watching and feeding the resident ducks.

Due to the high altitude, in the summer, the days are cool (70s) and the nighttime temperatures can be quite chilly (30s). The camp host sells firewood if you need to warm up in the evening. Fawn Lakes is a popular spot and will have several RVs, but it does have a tent-only loop.

Spruce, fir, river willow, and ponderosa pine shade most of the campsites, which are dirt and gravel. The tent loop includes sites 8–12, of which 8, 9, and 12 can be reserved. The best are two first-come, first-served sites: 10 and 11, which are close to the river and have the most seclusion and space. Site 12 is the only one in the tent loop that doesn't sit next to the river; instead, it backs up to the highway. Even though the highway lines one side of the campground, road noise is minimal, obscured by the sound of the rushing river. If you pitch your tent close to the riverbank, you likely won't hear the highway at all over the flowing water. In the campground section of the river, someone has built a small dam to pool water.

Families line the banks of Fawn Lakes to fish the weekend away.

KEY INFORMATION

LOCATION: NM 38, 12 miles east of Questa and 3 miles west of Red River

CONTACT: Carson National Forest, Questa Ranger District, 575-586-0520, tinyurl.com /fawnlakes; Concessionaire: Scenic Canyons, 435-245-6521, sceniccanyons.com

OPEN: Mid-May–Mid-September

SITES: 19

EACH SITE HAS: Picnic table, fire ring with grill

WHEELCHAIR ACCESS: Sites 14 and 16; accessible toilets and fishing

ASSIGNMENT: First-come, first-served (8 sites) or by reservation (877-444-6777, recreation .gov/camping/campgrounds/233388)

REGISTRATION: On-site or online

AMENITIES: Vault toilets, potable water from pumps

PARKING: At sites

FEE: $18/night ($9/night with Interagency Pass); $5/additional vehicle

ELEVATION: 8,483'

RESTRICTIONS

PETS: Allowed on leash

QUIET HOURS: 10 p.m.–6 a.m.

FIRES: In fire rings only

ALCOHOL: No restrictions

OTHER: 14-day stay limit; 8 people/site; check-in at noon, checkout at 2 p.m. No ATVs driven through camp. Firewood for sale with camp host.

While it's probably intended to make fishing easier, it actually makes a nice spot to dip your feet in, if you can tolerate the icy cold water.

There are three vault toilets: one by the entrance, one between two accessible sites (14 and 16), and one in the tent loop near site 12. Water spigots are conveniently situated throughout the camp, near the toilets. Even though the campground remains busy throughout summer, it stays clean.

You can fish right from your campsite or follow the short, paved path to the lakes. New Mexico Department of Game and Fish officials regularly stop by the lakes and check for fishing licenses and possession limits. The camp host asks that you not clean your fish in the vault toilets or at the water spigots (use the river or a wash tub at your site); keep dogs leashed and out of the lakes.

If you head into Red River, you can stop at the Town Hall and read the schedule detailing when the Red River Hatchery releases fish into the lakes and river. Built in 1941, the hatchery produces 1.7 million rainbow trout each year. They release 300 pounds of fish roughly once a week throughout the summer—when I visited, they had already released more than three tons of trout for the season. The camp host told me that some people follow the hatchery trucks from stop to stop until they've reached their possession limit (five fish per day). There's no need to resort to such extremes, though; the water is so clear in the river running through camp that you can see fish swimming.

The concessionaire has a relationship with Red River RV, which permits campers to use its coin-operated laundry and showers. There you can also purchase ice, or you can continue into town for more goods and services. In town you can find outfitters for almost every adventure: ATV rentals, horse rides, llama tours, and even day trips to pan for gold. Red River Brewery opened in 2018 and is one of the hot local spots. If you are traveling with children, the Red River Community House offers year-round family-friendly activities, including Movies on the Lawn, Music in the Mountains, daily hikes, craft hours, and science lessons.

You can often see fish swimming through the campground.

Fawn Lakes Campground

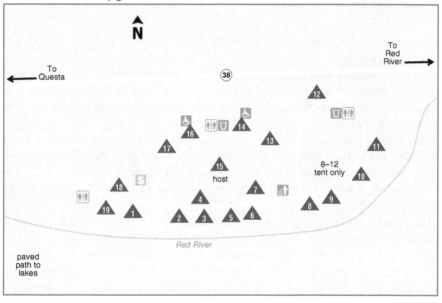

GETTING THERE

From Taos, drive north on NM 522 for 25 miles, until you reach Questa. Turn right on NM 38 and drive east for 9 miles. The campground will be on the right. It is 3.2 miles west of Red River.

GPS COORDINATES: N36° 42.422' W105° 26.910'

12

⛺ Fenton Lake State Park Campground

Beauty ★★★ Privacy ★★ Spaciousness ★★★ Quiet ★ Security ★★★★★ Cleanliness ★★★

The Rio Cebolla cuts west from Fenton Lake, and if you follow the cattails, that's where you'll find the campground.

In the 1976 sci-fi classic *The Man Who Fell to Earth,* a burning spaceship plummets from the clear, blue New Mexican sky into Fenton Lake. Instead of thin-hipped, lightning-striped Bowie starmen, Fenton Lake now hosts swarms of fishermen and their families. A beach near the picnic area sees most of the traffic: grandfathers pop open camping chairs and settle in to watch bobbers; small children play-fish at their feet or go for walks exploring the small lake. From ice fishing in the winter to kayaking in the summer, Fenton Lake never sees any downtime. The Rio Cebolla cuts west from the lake, and if you follow the cattails, that's where you'll find the campground.

Fenton Lake, like the other Jemez campgrounds, fills up fast nearly every day, so you'll need to plan early to pick the best sites. If you want to camp here, reserve a site or come bright and early to claim one of the first-come, first-served ones. Sites can be reserved six months in advance through reserveamerica.com but will be forfeited if the site is not occupied by 4 p.m.

The day-use area sometimes opens to overflow camping at Fenton Lake.

KEY INFORMATION

LOCATION: 455 Fenton Lake Rd.,
Jemez Springs, NM 87025

CONTACT: Fenton Lake State Park,
575-829-3630, emnrd.state.nm.us/SPD
/fentonlakestatepark.html

OPEN: Year-round

SITES: 36

EACH SITE HAS: Picnic table, fire ring

WHEELCHAIR ACCESS: The group site,
sites 6A and 6B, parking, restrooms, and
fishing are all accessible.

ASSIGNMENT: First-come, first-served and
by reservation (877-664-7787,
newmexicostateparks.reserveamerica.com)

REGISTRATION: On-site or online
(with printed receipt)

AMENITIES: Vault toilets, group site and group
picnic shelter, boat ramp

PARKING: At sites

FEE: $10/night for camping; $30/night for
group site; $6/day for the day-use area.
The New Mexico State Parks Annual Camping Pass waives the $10/night camping fee.

ELEVATION: 7,624'

RESTRICTIONS

PETS: Allowed on leashes up to 10 feet long;
do not leave pets unattended

QUIET HOURS: 10 p.m.–7 a.m.

FIRES: In fire rings only

ALCOHOL: Permitted

OTHER: 14-day stay limit; checkout is at
2 p.m. Memorial Day, Labor Day, and
the Fourth of July weekend require a
3-night minimum stay if arriving that
Friday and a 2-night minimum stay if
arriving that Saturday.

Loop D and sites 1, 5, 6A, 9, 11, 17, and 29 are reservation areas. When I visited, the rangers had opened up Loop C, part of the day-use area, as camping overflow. Loop C, needless to say, is not the best camping option—there's no privacy, little space, and no escape from the buzzing day-use area.

Loop D forms the RV section, which has electric hookups. The campground doesn't have a dump station. Following the Rio Cebolla and the road, you can get away from RVs quickly; Loop F is the farthest away from generators.

Site 14 shares an island of grass and trees with the playground; they're so close, in fact, that the play structure feels like it's part of the site. This site would be ideal for a family with kids—where else do you get to camp in a playground?

For those wanting privacy and more space between tents, head to sites 16, 17, and 18. A hiking trail—the 2-mile-long Hal Baxter Memorial Trail and Biathlon Practice Area—starts across the road from site 18. It leads you back to the lake, dead-ending at the Lake Fork Day Use Area. Sites 9, 11, 14, 17, 29, and 30 are close to the river. Each loop has its own vault toilet.

You're not allowed to swim in the lake. You may, however, take a canoe, kayak, rowboat, or small Class A boat (under 16 feet with an electric trolling motor) out on the water. The water level drops up to 18 inches in the fall due to evaporation and rises in the spring with the snowmelt runoff. On the west side of the lake, there's shoreline and ADA fishing pads that meet the water's edge.

Several signs posted in the campground warn that a cougar has been spotted in the area. The cougar likely won't come down to the lake, even with the promise of rainbow, German, and brown trout, because it's so packed with people. Take caution, however, when hiking in the hills above the lake, particularly at dawn and dusk.

Fenton Lake is very secure: in addition to a camp host, New Mexico State Parks has a staffed office in the day-use area. Rangers patrol constantly, ensuring that everyone has paid for camping or picnicking, and that you have a fishing license if you have a rod and reel in hand. If you need a fishing license, you can purchase one up in La Cueva, 8 miles back down NM 126. There you'll find a bait-and-tackle general store, a family-run restaurant, and outdoor-recreation rentals.

If you have children under the age of 11, they can also fish for free at the kids' pond at Seven Springs Hatchery. This hatchery is responsible for breeding and distributing native Rio Grande cutthroat trout, which is New Mexico's state fish. Since 2002 it has raised more than 72,000 trout for stocking our lakes and rivers. To get there, drive about 3 miles past Fenton Lake and turn right onto Forest Service Road 314.

For dinner at the saloon, a massage at the bathhouse, or a soak in a managed hot spring, you'll have to return to Jemez Springs. The nearest gas stations are in Jemez Pueblo, about 31 miles south, or Los Alamos, 39 miles east.

Fenton Lake State Park Campground

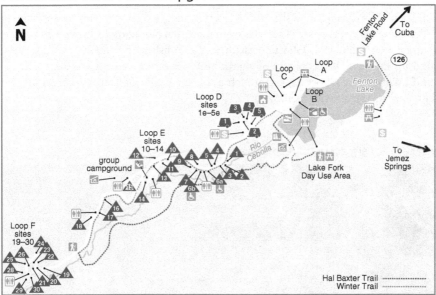

GETTING THERE

From the intersection of NM 4 and Mooney Boulevard in Jemez Springs, drive north 8.5 miles on NM 4 and turn left (northwest) on NM 126. In 9.4 miles, turn left onto Fenton Lake Road to reach the campground.

GPS COORDINATES: N35° 52.916' W106° 43.750'

13

⛺ Holy Ghost Campground

Beauty ★★★★★ Privacy ★★★ Spaciousness ★★★ Quiet ★★★ Security ★★ Cleanliness ★★★

Mule deer nibble pink roses off their stems and bats glide across the sky at this campground.

As evening settled and I started a campfire, a doe and her fawn wandered down the hill and started browsing our site. Many of the campsites at Holy Ghost are surrounded by knee-high grass and thickets of wild roses; our site (23) also had a chokecherry bush in fragrant bloom. While mule deer like chokecherries, it was the roses these two were after. They spent nearly 30 minutes nipping pink blossoms off of the bushes before an off-leash dog scared them back up the hill. After they left, I noticed the bats gliding out of the fir trees, plucking mayflies from midair.

Encounters like these are why so many people return to Holy Ghost Campground; I spoke with many campers who came here year after year and refused to camp anywhere else in Pecos. The campground shows its age: crumbling asphalt glows in the moonlight; the U.S. Forest Service has removed handles from the rust-colored midcentury water pumps to discourage use. While Holy Ghost doesn't have the polish of the larger Jack's Creek Campground up the road, it has plenty of charm and is a beautiful camping spot. The campground follows Holy Ghost Creek through a narrow valley, flanked by steep hills. Spruce and fir trees fill the air with their scent.

Deer browse the campsites at Holy Ghost Campground.

KEY INFORMATION

LOCATION: FS 122, Terrero, NM 87573

CONTACT: Santa Fe National Forest, Pecos/
Las Vegas Ranger District, 505-438-5300,
tinyurl.com/holyghostcampground

OPEN: May–October, depending on weather

SITES: 23, including 1 camp host site

EACH SITE HAS: Picnic table, fire ring

WHEELCHAIR ACCESS: Accessible toilets;
at least 1 accessible site

ASSIGNMENT: First-come, first-served;
no reservations

REGISTRATION: Self-register at entrance

AMENITIES: Vault toilets, trash bins

PARKING: At sites; 5 walk-in sites share a
parking lot

FEE: $8/night ($4 with Interagency Pass)

ELEVATION: 8,154'

RESTRICTIONS

PETS: Allowed on leash

QUIET HOURS: 10 p.m.–7 a.m.

FIRES: In fire rings only

ALCOHOL: Permitted

OTHER: 14-day stay limit; no horses, horse
trailers, or ATVs; maximum 3 vehicles/site

Four sets of vault toilets are relatively new and clean. They can get muddy after many visits by people wading in the creek, but the rangers appear to hose them down occasionally. Evidently there was once potable water here, but the Forest Service recommends against using the old pumps. Best to bring your own or filter it from the creek.

Site 1 is the camp host site, but when I visited, none was on duty. Instead a family occupied it for day use, and when evening fell another family set up camp. If you can snag it, this is a great location, with several trees and creek access. If you don't mind lugging your kit to the walk-in sites, site 13 is gorgeous. Completely hidden by a stand of young aspen, the path for this site starts just past the locked gate for the group site. Site 15 has the longest access trail, up a little hill overlooking sites 14 and 11. Sites 2–10 border the creek; sites 17–24 back up to the hill. On the creek side, you can often set up in the trees. Site 24 is near the entrance, but it's also spacious enough to be a double site.

The group area, which you can rent for $50 per night April–November, has a ramada with several picnic tables, a group campfire area, and a large pedestal grill. It can accommodate up to 40 people. A paved path hugs the creek's bank and provides pullouts with fishing access.

I did see a snake near one of the toilets. It looked like a young, harmless garter snake, but it's best to take precautions and watch where you step. Remember that most snakes are usually harmless unless provoked. While a camp host was not assigned to Holy Ghost in the summer of 2019, the rangers drove through regularly to keep an eye on the campground.

You won't see many RVs in this campground. The forest road to get here is narrow and winding, with several one-lane bridges and shallow potholes. Most RVs instead head to Jack's Creek Campground for the night or pack into the G.A.I.N. (Gaining Access into Nature) parking lots that line NM 63. These state-run wildlife-management areas overflow on summer weekends. They require permits that can be purchased from the New Mexico Department of Game and Fish.

Backpackers and hikers start their adventures at the parking lot by the campground's entrance. Across from the lot, Holy Ghost Trail 283 starts. Many hikers choose to postpone this initial calf workout and instead walk through the campground and pick up the trail behind the group area. There, the trail crisscrosses the creek, and hikers can practice their balance on downed trees and log bridges. A popular, if steep, hike connects with Trail 254 to Stewart Lake (about 7 miles). Other backpackers continue on to Lake Katherine or Spirit Lake for an escape into the high alpine forests of the Pecos Wilderness. The clear, turquoise waters of Lake Katherine, with Santa Fe Baldy in the background, make this a favorite hike of many New Mexicans. Some trails go into a burned area; hazards include falling trees, flash flooding and debris flows, and portions of trails that may be blocked or damaged.

The closest gas stations, convenience stores, fishing licenses, and tacos are in Pecos. Terrero, at the split on NM 63 and Forest Service Road 122, does have a small general store but no gas.

Holy Ghost Campground

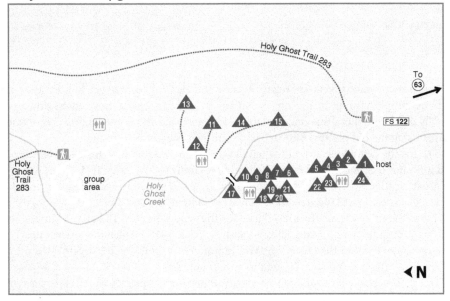

GETTING THERE

From I-25 in Santa Fe, take Exit 299 toward Glorieta/Pecos. Turn left (east) onto NM 50 and continue 6 miles to Pecos; then turn left (north) onto NM 63 (North Main Street). After 13 miles, the road forks at Terrero; turn left (northeast) onto FS 122 (Holy Ghost Canyon Road) and continue for about 3 miles. The road ends at the campground.

GPS COORDINATES: N35° 46.564' W105° 42.159'

14

⛺ Hopewell Lake Campground

Beauty ★★★ Privacy ★★★★ Spaciousness ★★★★ Quiet ★★★ Security ★★★ Cleanliness ★★★★

Fishing isn't the only draw—hikers and horseback riders also flock to Hopewell Lake Campground, as the Continental Divide National Scenic Trail passes through the area, skirting the southern shore of the lake.

Between Tres Piedras and Tierra Amarilla lies a 14-acre lake heralded as some of the best still-water fishing in Northern New Mexico. Regularly stocked with rainbow and brook trout, Hopewell Lake draws a bigger crowd than nearby Canjilon Lakes. Hopewell is large enough, too, to spend the day drifting off-shore in a canoe or raft. According to the U.S. Forest Service, you can fish from the shore, from a motorized boat, or from a float tube; you can fly-fish, use spinners, or load up your hook with bait. The day-use area at the lake has picnic tables and grills, so you can hook and cook your trout in the same afternoon. Fishing, however, isn't the only draw—hikers and horseback riders also flock to Hopewell Lake, as the Continental Divide National Scenic Trail goes through the campground, skirting the southern shore of the water.

The scenic drive along NM 64 to reach this man-made lake takes you through rolling hills of conifers and aspen, rarely dipping below 9,500 feet in elevation. Parts of this highway close during the winter due to heavy snows. When the campground opens, these high

Hopewell Lake is a popular stop along the Continental Divide National Scenic Trail.

KEY INFORMATION

LOCATION: US 64, about 20 miles east of Tres Piedras

CONTACT: Carson National Forest, Tres Piedras Ranger District, 575-758-8678, tinyurl.com/hopewell-lake; Scenic Canyons (concessionaire), 435-245-6521, sceniccanyons.com/hopewell-lake.html

OPEN: Memorial Day–Labor Day

SITES: 31, plus 1 group site

EACH SITE HAS: Picnic table, fire ring

WHEELCHAIR ACCESS: Accessible toilets

ASSIGNMENT: First-come, first-served and by reservation (877-444-6777, recreation.gov /camping/campgrounds/233327)

REGISTRATION: Self-register on-site or online

AMENITIES: Vault toilets, horse corrals and water troughs, group day-use shelter

PARKING: At sites

FEE: $20/night individual sites; $16/night with an Interagency Pass; $100/night group site; $5/additional vehicle

ELEVATION: 9,883'

RESTRICTIONS

PETS: Allowed on leash

QUIET HOURS: 10 p.m.–6 a.m.

FIRES: In fire rings only

ALCOHOL: Permitted at sites only

OTHER: Off-road vehicles are allowed in the area but must be trailered in and out of the campground; checkout 1 p.m. Cell coverage is poor here.

meadows are still patchy with snow and cold enough to scare off all but the hardiest tent campers. Once the weather warms, wildflowers bloom throughout the meadows: red clover, purplish fleabane, and bright yellow cinquefoils dominate.

This campground fills up on holiday weekends and just before school starts back in late summer. An annual July tent revival rents out not only the group site but also sites 21–32. About half of the sites are reservable online, if you're nervous about grabbing a spot. Near the entrance, all of the sites are bunched together (particularly sites 1–8), but they start to spread out nearer to the horse corrals. Sites 16 and 17 have established corrals; 17 even has a water trough. Site 13 had a temporary corral set up when I visited; at site 15, campers had hung a string line between two trees for their horses. Site 21 is the gem of the campground, set far back from the road in a large meadow, with some shady evergreens. You almost forget you're sharing the campground with so many fellow campers! Four vault toilets are spaced throughout the loop; each is accompanied by trash bins and water spigots. Chainsaw crews have been working in the nearby forest, filling up the campsites with free firewood. In seasons without these crews, a truck from the concessionaire drives through the campground on the weekends selling firewood.

West of the lake, you can explore ruins of the town of Hopewell, which was named for rancher and promoter Willard S. Hopewell. The town had a post office from 1894 to 1906— gold-bearing quartz veins were discovered there in the 1870s, hence the name of Placer Creek. You can pick up the Continental Divide Trail between sites 16 and 17 and walk it down to the lake. The whole trail meanders for 820 miles through New Mexico alone, but it doesn't always exactly follow the divide. It skirts reservations and crosses State Trust Lands, which require a special $35 permit from the State Lands Office. Near Hopewell Lake, the trail is rated as easy, with elevation highs of 10,515 feet and lows of 9,489 feet. The cool, dry weather of Carson National Forest makes this a nice access point to hike a portion of the trail. At this altitude, you can expect brisk nights and cool summer days. Pack plenty of layers. If you're coming from a much lower altitude, you may want to familiarize yourself with the signs of altitude sickness and the best ways to acclimatize. In the summer, be prepared for afternoon monsoon rains.

Tres Piedras is the closest town, only 20 miles east; Tierra Amarilla is 30 miles away. Take caution while driving on NM 64 and NM 84; lots of deer live here. While I was researching this site in midafternoon, a deer bolted out of the sagebrush and hit my car, totaling it. In addition to deer, you may see elk and black bears.

Hopewell Lake Campground

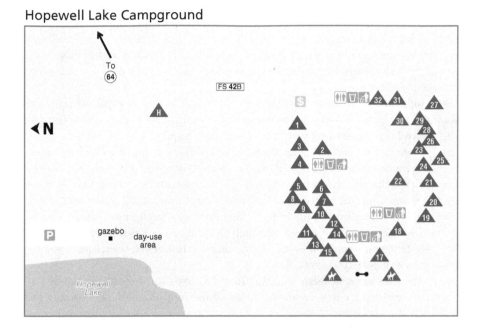

GETTING THERE

From Española, take US 84 West toward Chama, and in 7.4 miles bear right onto US 285 North. After 47 miles, turn left onto US 64 West. Continue for 19 miles; the campground will be on your left.

GPS COORDINATES: N36° 42.084' W106° 13.991'

15

Iron Gate Campground

Beauty ★★★★★ Privacy ★★★★ Spaciousness ★★★★★ Quiet ★★★★★ Security ★★★ Cleanliness ★★★

Every so often a break in the trees permits a stunning view of the snowcapped mountains in the southern tail of the Rockies.

If you're looking for a campground that offers a bit of solitude in an alpine forest, Iron Gate is for you. Due to the difficult access to this campground, people come only if they really want to be here. On a summer weekend, only half the sites were occupied. You'll hear no generators because no RVs come to this remote location. The campground is silent save for the wind through the quaking aspen, busy woodpeckers, the crackle of your campfire, and other relaxing sounds of nature.

The 4 miles up Forest Service Road 223, also known as Iron Gate Road, are rough; due to rocks and ruts, I highly recommend driving a high-clearance vehicle up to the campground. While the road was dusty and dry when I visited, I can imagine how difficult it would be taking a regular four-door sedan there in the mud—you'd be certain to knock a hole in your oil pan. During monsoon season, the road may become impassable. That said, the drive is quite scenic. You pass through the summer homes of Grass Mountain, and every so often a break in the trees permits a stunning view of the snow-capped mountains in the southern tail of the Rockies. Mule deer browse roadside, picking their way through lush meadows covered in wildflowers. You may even see elk. The high alpine forest grows thicker and wilder each mile. By the time you reach Iron Gate Campground, the fir trees have such girth you can tell they must be well over 100 years old.

All of the sites are spaciously situated around a single loop; many are amply shaded. The sites closer to the entrance on the inside of the loop (12 and 14) lack any privacy

Make sure to stop for spectacular views on the way to Iron Gate Campground.

LOCATION: FR 223 (Iron Gate Road), about 23 miles north of Pecos

CONTACT: Santa Fe National Forest, Pecos/ Las Vegas Ranger District, 505-438-5300, tinyurl.com/irongatecampground

OPEN: May–October, depending on weather

SITES: 14, including 2 walk-in sites

EACH SITE HAS: Picnic table, fire ring

WHEELCHAIR ACCESS: Accessible toilets; at least 1 accessible site

ASSIGNMENT: First-come, first-served; no reservations

REGISTRATION: Self-register at entrance

AMENITIES: Vault toilets, trash bins, horse corrals; no potable water

PARKING: At sites

FEE: $4/night ($2 with Interagency Pass)

ELEVATION: 9,472'

RESTRICTIONS

PETS: Allowed on leash

QUIET HOURS: 10 p.m.–7 a.m.

FIRES: In fire rings only

ALCOHOL: At campsites only

OTHER: 14-day maximum stay; no ATVs; maximum 3 cars/site; maximum recommended length for vehicle with a horse trailer attached is 30'

afforded by trees. They sit in an open meadow of dandelions and wild irises. Sites 6 and 13 have corrals nearby, which may mean more flies during wetter months. Sites 2, 6, 7, and 8 exemplify the potential for campground tent camping to be both beautiful and secluded. Sites 7 and 8 are walk-in and near a trailhead that leads from the campground down to the Pecos River and Panchuela.

None of the sites have tent pads, but they do have several good locations to pitch tents. The toilets were clean but had a strong odor. You may want to bring your own roll of toilet paper, as the restrooms seem to have weekly care and may run out of TP during busy camping weekends. The trash bins are not bear-proof, but that doesn't mean wild animals don't visit this remote campground. No camp host was on duty during the summer of 2019, but the rangers stopped by frequently to check on the area and its temporary inhabitants.

At an elevation of 9,400 feet, you can expect brisk nights and cool summer days. Pack plenty of layers. If you're coming from a much lower altitude, you may want to familiarize yourself with the signs of altitude sickness and the best ways to acclimatize. There is no potable water in this campground and no easy creek or river access that many of the other Pecos campgrounds enjoy. Come prepared with enough water to drown your campfire in addition to the amount you'll need to drink, wash dishes, and so on—at least 5 gallons.

One popular day hike from the campground goes to the grassy Hamilton Mesa, which offers views of the surrounding mountains (Trail 249). If you're backpacking this trail, you can follow it to a junction that leads you to Pecos Falls. Camping in the vicinity of Pecos Falls is prohibited, however. Another day hike to Mora Flats follows a ridgeline to the Rio Valdez (Trail 250). Some trails go into a burned area; hazards include falling trees, flash flooding and debris flows, and portions of trails that may be blocked or damaged.

The closest gas stations, convenience stores, fishing licenses, and tacos are in Pecos. Terrero, at the split on NM 63 and Forest Service Road 122, does have a small general store but no gas. Mileage-wise they aren't that far from the campground, but over FS 223 it will take a long time to get there, so it's best to come prepared with all necessary supplies.

Wildflowers bloom beneath the fir and spruce trees at Iron Gate.

Iron Gate Campground

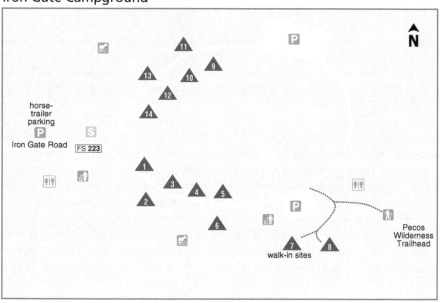

GETTING THERE

From I-25 in Santa Fe, take Exit 299 toward Glorieta/Pecos. Turn left (east) onto NM 50 and continue 6 miles to Pecos; then turn left (north) onto NM 63 (North Main Street). After 18 miles, bear right (northeast) onto FS 223 (Iron Gate Road). After 4 miles, the road dead-ends at the campground.

GPS COORDINATES: N35° 50.399' W105° 37.238'

16

△ Jemez Falls Campground

Beauty ★★★★★ Privacy ★★★★ Spaciousness ★★★★★ Quiet ★★★★ Security ★★★★ Cleanliness ★★★★

Among the lush forest meadows, towering ponderosa pines, and breathtaking vistas of the Jemez Mountains, you'll find this shady campground.

Following NM 4 through the Jemez Mountains, you soon enter the lush forest meadows, towering ponderosa pines, and breathtaking vistas that draw so many weekenders from Albuquerque and Santa Fe to the Santa Fe National Forest. In the middle of this lovely panorama, you'll find Jemez Falls Campground, completely forested with ponderosa pines.

Foresters call young ponderosa pines "blackjacks" because they have black, rough bark. As ponderosa pines age, their bark becomes orange and smooth, with fine flakes. In some areas, you may see where dense stands of blackjacks have been thinned to prevent forest fires and to open the canopy to help other trees grow. These downed blackjacks may be used in poles, vigas (roofing logs), and fence posts, adding to the charm of New Mexican architecture. Camping at Jemez Falls, you'll quickly notice the beautiful, mature orange pines mixed with blackjacks. They shade the rolling, grassy hills of the campground and provide support for hammocks. The U.S. Forest Service has let some stands of blackjacks continue to grow around campsites to create more privacy.

Jemez Falls are the highest waterfalls in the Jemez Mountains.

KEY INFORMATION

LOCATION: Off NM 4, about 15 miles northeast of Jemez Springs

CONTACT: Santa Fe National Forest, Jemez Ranger District, 575-829-3535, tinyurl.com/jemezfalls

OPEN: Mid-May–mid-September

SITES: 51

EACH SITE HAS: Picnic table, fire ring

ASSIGNMENT: By reservation only mid-May–September (877-444-6777, recreation.gov /camping/campgrounds/274315); first-come, first-served sites sometimes available in the off-season

REGISTRATION: Check in with camp host upon arrival

AMENITIES: Vault toilets, drinking water, and dumpsters at each loop

PARKING: At sites

FEE: $10/night (per vehicle)

ELEVATION: 8,008'

RESTRICTIONS

PETS: Allowed on leash

QUIET HOURS: 10 p.m.–6 a.m.

FIRES: In fire rings only

ALCOHOL: Permitted

OTHER: 14-night stay limit; maximum 3 vehicles/site; check-in at 3 p.m., checkout at 2 p.m.; no ATVs or OHVs allowed. Dead and downed wood in the forest can be picked up for firewood. No shooting firearms, BB guns, slingshots, wrist rockets, or archery bows.

Jemez Falls, like the other Jemez campgrounds, fills up fast nearly every day, so you'll need to plan early to pick the best sites—the camp host told me that many of the sites are booked six months in advance, particularly for weekends. This campground and many others in the area recently switched to reservation-only due to their heavy use. You may be able to walk in a month before and a month after the campground is officially open (that is, early May and October); contact the Jemez Ranger District for details. Jemez Falls is nonelectric, but long RVs can fit in most of the sites, so don't be surprised to see several vehicles larger than the official reading material suggests.

The campground is divided into four loops, each with a vault toilet, a water spigot, and a dumpster. Site 47, the so-called honeymoon suite, is especially popular because it's the farthest out on loop 4 and doesn't have any neighbors. Other popular sites are 35, which has a neat pile of boulders, and 26, which backs up to a hill. Site 46 sits downhill from a set of ruins; check them out, but don't disturb the grounds or take anything. Loop 1 sites are the most spacious, with lots of room between sites.

From the campground, it's a half-mile walk to the fishing day-use area and about a quarter mile to the Jemez Falls overlook. You can pick up the trail by site 48. The waterfall is the largest in the Jemez Mountains, and upstream there's a nice, small beach that's perfect for a picnic or wading in the water.

Behind site 28, a path leads to Trail 137; if you turn left, you'll head to the waterfall, and if you turn right, you'll find yourself at McCauley Warm Springs and eventually, Battleship Rock. The warm springs are 84°F, and you may find yourself soaking in the pool with guppies and neon tetras. The bridge at Trail 137 near Jemez Falls washed out in 2018; hike with caution if it hasn't been replaced yet.

In addition to the pines, the campground is dotted with yellow and white wildflowers throughout the summer: you'll see clusters of yellow mountain parsley, sparsely petalled yellow groundsels, woolly and white small-leaf pussytoes, and those cheery yellow-and-white trailing fleabanes. Elk, foxes, and coyotes also enjoy this campground, as do hummingbirds.

Unfortunately, *Ips* beetles (also known as engraver beetles) and mountain pine beetles also love these stunning ponderosa forests. These beetles have killed significant numbers of trees throughout the Southwest and increase the possibility of forest fires both on the ground and through the canopy. It's due to these beetles that while you can collect and burn any downed and dead wood you find in the campground, the rangers ask that you not take any wood out of the campground, as you may help spread beetles.

Santa Fe National Forest has been hit hard by forest fires these last few decades. One in 2007 nearly burned down this campground; the Las Conchas Fire of 2011 burned over 156,000 acres and was the state's largest wildfire in recorded history. You can still see its devastation along NM 4. While the Las Conchas Fire started from a tree falling onto a power line, it's still a good reminder to practice fire safety.

If you find you've forgotten anything, Amanda's Jemez Mountain Country Store in La Cueva, 6 miles west on NM 4, at the turn off for NM 126, might have it. For dinner, a massage, or a soak in a managed hot spring, you'll have to return to Jemez Springs. The nearest gas stations are in Jemez Pueblo, about 27 miles south, or Los Alamos, 25 miles east.

Jemez Falls Campground

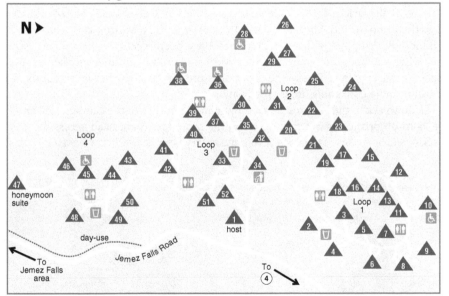

GETTING THERE

From Jemez Springs, head northeast on NM 4 East for 14 miles. When you see the campground sign on the right, turn right (south) onto Jemez Falls Road. The campground is just shy of a mile down this road.

GPS COORDINATES: N35° 49.439' W106° 36.384'

17

⛺ Paliza Family Campground

Beauty ★★★★★ Privacy ★★★★ Spaciousness ★★★★★ Quiet ★★★★ Security ★★★★★ Cleanliness ★★★★★

Stay at the original base camp for the CCC in Santa Fe National Forest.

Paliza Family Campground is a beautiful facility near Jemez Springs. While other nearby campgrounds—such as San Antonio and Fenton Lake—fill up fast on the weekends, Paliza Family Campground offers an alternative that lies just far enough off the beaten path to deliver a great, quiet camping experience. Between the magnificent ponderosa pines that smell of vanilla when you walk past and thickets of wild roses, this is a fragrant site. Hummingbirds zip through the roses, and Abert's squirrels dart up and down the pines.

Paliza Creek separates the campground from Forest Service Road 10 on one side; a smaller creek runs alongside the opposite side. Along with the frogs and watercress of the lush riparian ecosystem, you'll also find a lot of poison ivy on the banks of the creek. Take caution by wearing long socks, pants, and long sleeves—and of course, when you see leaves of three, let it be.

Three of the original 1930s Civilian Conservation Corps base-camp buildings are still at the campground. Sites 6, 13, and 15 each have CCC Adirondack lean-tos. These log buildings, equipped with stone fireplaces, have been recently restored and warm up nicely when you get a fire going. They are ideal shelters for summer monsoon rains and crisp, early fall evenings. Due to the elevation, summer days may be warm, but the nights can still be quite cool and a fire is appreciated.

The drawback to the lean-tos is that they sit in the middle of the campground and don't have as much privacy as other sites. For a little more seclusion, head across the creek to sites 3, 4, and 5—to reach these sites, you must carry your gear down a few stone steps and

A short hike takes you to the towering hoodoos at the Goblin Colony.

KEY INFORMATION

LOCATION: FS 10, Ponderosa, NM 87044

CONTACT: Santa Fe National Forest, Jemez Ranger District, 575-829-3535, tinyurl.com/palizacampground

OPEN: Early May–mid-October

SITES: 30 sites; another campground nearby has group sites

EACH SITE HAS: Picnic table, lantern pole, and fire ring; some sites have additional picnic tables and a pedestal grill; 3 sites have Adirondack lean-tos

WHEELCHAIR ACCESS: Accessible restrooms

ASSIGNMENT: First-come, first-served; no reservations

REGISTRATION: At entrance

AMENITIES: Vault toilets; no dump station, drinking water, or electricity

PARKING: At sites

FEE: $8/night (per vehicle; $4 with Interagency Pass)

ELEVATION: 6,726'

RESTRICTIONS

PETS: Permitted on leash

QUIET HOURS: 10 p.m.–6 a.m.

FIRES: In fire rings only

ALCOHOL: Permitted

OTHER: 14-day stay limit; check-in at 3 p.m., checkout at 2 p.m.; sites must be occupied the first night of a reservation and cannot be left unoccupied for more than 24 hours; maximum 2 vehicles/site. Because the last 2 miles of the road to the campground are rough dirt, the U.S. Forest Service recommends driving high-clearance vehicles.

---

across a delightful rock bridge. Set off from the rest of the campground, these renovated tent sites feel like they're in a world of their own.

I camped here during an hour-long downpour, and while the lean-tos looked cozy and inviting, I didn't have any problems with water pooling or flooding at my site. The whole campground is sloped in Lower Paliza Canyon, which helps control water during summer storms.

Most of the sites are constructed for one tent, but there are seven double sites—even one triple (site 21)—along the second loop. The group site down the road can accommodate up to 100 people. The fee station and camp host are at the entrance of the campground. Four vault toilets are equally spaced throughout the grounds—with two in the main loop and one in each of the other loops. There's no potable water here, but you can buy water at Jemez Pueblo, and Jemez Springs offers additional services and food options. Still, it's best to come prepared with your own supplies.

Between sites 21 and 22, a short interpretive trail has a bench where you can rest and enjoy the hummingbirds or evening chorus of frogs. Near site 29, a hiking trail takes you across the creek into the wilderness. If you continue on FS 10 for 2 miles, you'll come to a trail marker for the Goblin Colony, a collection of hoodoos; the marker is easy to miss, just past a DROWN CAMPFIRES sign, on the right side of the road. These hoodoos, formed from volcanic ash, have eroded into interesting—goblin-resembling, perhaps—shapes, pock-marked with holes. While hoodoos cover about 30 acres, no real trails exist, leaving you free to wander through the interesting formations. (For more information about this hike, check out *60 Hikes Within 60 Miles: Albuquerque* by David Ryan and Stephen Ausherman.) Near the Goblin Colony, you may find the ruins of Boletsakwa Pueblo, a historic refuge pueblo dating to the 1680s. You may also find petroglyphs of humanlike figures. Be gentle with the fragile hoodoos—they aren't as solid as they appear—and leave all artifacts in place.

If you head back to Jemez Pueblo and drive north on NM 4, you'll quickly reach the popular weekend spots that draw scores of people to the Jemez area every weekend—hiking one of the many trailheads just off the highway, fishing in Jemez River or Fenton Lake, or soaking in the numerous hot springs.

Paliza Family Campground

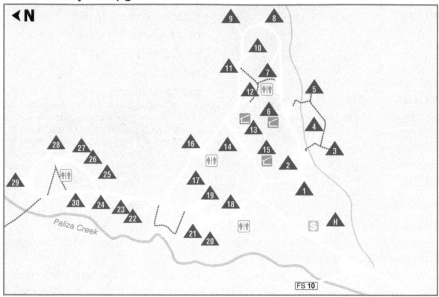

GETTING THERE

From I-25 in Bernalillo, take Exit 242 onto US 550 North. In 23.5 miles, turn right (northeast) onto NM 4 North. In 6.2 miles, just after Jemez Pueblo, turn right (east) onto NM 290/FS 10, and continue 4 miles. Past Ponderosa Valley Vineyards, the road will turn to dirt for the last 2 miles before you reach Paliza Family Campground, on the right.

GPS COORDINATES: N35° 42.239' W106° 37.567'

⛺ Panchuela Campground

Beauty ★★★★ Privacy ★★★★ Spaciousness ★★★★★ Quiet ★★★★★ Security ★★★ Cleanliness ★★★

At Panchuela Campground, you can witness the effect that dandelions, golden pea, and lovely purple Rocky Mountain irises have on pollinators.

In *Braiding Sweetgrass*, botanist Robin Wall Kimmerer writes that she wanted to study biology in order to learn why purple and gold flowers look so good together. As it turns out, this color combination is not only complementary, but we have special cones in our eyes that receive the light from just those two colors. Bees are similarly attracted to the combination of purple and yellow; a meadow filled with flowers of these colors will have more bees and butterflies. At Panchuela Campground, you can witness the effect that dandelions, golden pea, and lovely purple Rocky Mountain irises have on pollinators. Dozens of butterflies flutter from purple to gold petals. When I visited, a hummingbird zipped from one iris to the next, making its way through the alpine meadow sipping nectar as it went.

In addition to the abundant wildflowers and their visitors, Panchuela Campground has plenty of fir and spruce to shade campsites, lend privacy, and support hammocks. The campground in this gorgeous little canyon is small but stunning. The hills around it block the sun early in the evening and until late in the morning, making it a nice summer escape and great for late sleepers. The sites are tent-only, and you must pack your coolers, tents, and other items from the parking lot down to your site, but the walk isn't that far—about 100 yards at most.

Meadows in the Pecos Wilderness explode with wildflowers each summer.

KEY INFORMATION

LOCATION: Panchuela Rd.,
about 22 miles north of Pecos

CONTACT: Santa Fe National Forest, Pecos/
Las Vegas Ranger District, 505-438-5300,
tinyurl.com/panchuela

OPEN: May–October, depending on weather

SITES: 6

EACH SITE HAS: Picnic table, fire ring;
3 sites have Adirondack lean-tos

WHEELCHAIR ACCESS: Accessible parking
and restrooms

ASSIGNMENT: First-come, first-served;
no reservations

REGISTRATION: Self-register at parking lot

AMENITIES: Vault toilet, trash bin;
no potable water

PARKING: Parking lot near entrance

FEE: $5/night ($2.50 with Interagency Pass)

ELEVATION: 8,371'

RESTRICTIONS

PETS: Permitted on leash

QUIET HOURS: 10 p.m.–7 a.m.

FIRES: In fire rings only

ALCOHOL: Permitted

OTHER: Tent camping only; no horse trailers
allowed; no ATVs; 14-day stay limit

Three sites have Adirondack shelters, which are three-sided structures with stone fireplaces. They make nice shade on warm summer afternoons and great shelter during monsoon season. If you wanted to, you could hang a tarp over the exposed side and ditch the tent altogether. The two sites at the end of the trail that have Adirondack shelters are especially nice. Otherwise I would recommend the first site to the left as you enter—it's up a little hill and so obscured by trees that I nearly missed it entirely.

The campground has one restroom shared among the six sites; another vault toilet, which is accessible, is at the parking lot. This lot fills with cars on the weekends, as it doubles

as the parking area for fishermen, day hikers, and backpackers entering the Pecos Wilderness from the Panchuela Trailhead (note that there are only 19 parking spaces). While the campground can be very active during the day with these visitors, it empties at sunset. There is a campsite at the parking lot that appears to be a host site, but when I visited, no one was on duty.

Panchuela Creek runs alongside the campground; it forks at Cave Creek and again at Rito Perro. If you cross the creek, you can take a network of trails (288 to 251 to 267) to Lake Johnson near Redondo Peak. Cave Creek is a popular fishing spot.

If you strike out finding a site at Panchuela and want to camp in a nearby meadow that's

Watch for hummingbirds visiting
the wild irises near your campsite.

also filled with golden and purple flowers, Cowles Campground is just south on NM 63. Cowles has 10 sites but little privacy; the sites share a vault toilet and trash bins at the parking lot. Two sites with Adirondack shelters line the side of the parking lot. The others are walk-in, via a short trail, and share a meadow without many trees or bushes to surround your campsite.

From the campground, another short trail leads you down to Cowles Ponds. These two stocked ponds are fun for kids. A smaller pond is kids-only; you must be under age 12 or have an ADA license to fish there (the pond does have an accessible dock). Nearby Lisboa Springs Fish Hatchery, built in 1921 and the oldest hatchery in the state, produces some 65,000 pounds of sterile rainbow trout every year to stock this pond and nearby creeks. Remember to pack out fishing line. The U.S. Forest Service asks that if you do wade into the creeks to fish, clean your gear and your shoes to prevent the spread of whirling disease. This disease, caused by a parasite, places pressure on the fish's organ of equilibrium, causing it to swim in circles or whirl. Don't worry, though: humans can't get the parasite, so even if you catch a fish from infested waters, you should be safe.

The closest gas stations, convenience stores, fishing licenses, or tacos are in Pecos. Terrero, at the split on NM 63 and Forest Service Road 122, has a small general store but no gas.

Panchuela Campground

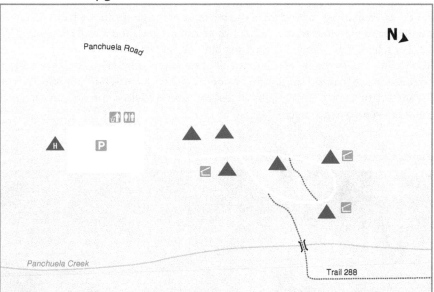

GETTING THERE

From I-25 in Santa Fe, take Exit 299 toward Glorieta/Pecos. Turn left (east) onto NM 50 and continue 6 miles to Pecos; then turn left (north) onto NM 63 (North Main Street). After 19 miles, make a slight left onto Windsor Road; then, in 0.2 mile, turn right (north) onto Panchuela Road. The road will dead-end after 1.5 miles; there you'll see the parking lot for the campground.

GPS COORDINATES: N35° 49.834' W105° 39.890'

19

⛺ Rio Chama Campground

Beauty ★★★★★ Privacy ★★★★★ Spaciousness ★★★★ Quiet ★★★★★ Security ★★★★ Cleanliness ★★★★

In nearly every direction, cliffs reveal a rainbow of strata—red, pink, purple, green, yellow, white, brown.

On the road to Rio Chama Campground, you can see why artists such as Georgia O'Keeffe have been drawn to New Mexico. In nearly every direction, cliffs reveal a rainbow of strata—red, pink, purple, green, yellow, white, brown. With this incredible view, the 12 miles of gravel road that you travel to reach Rio Chama Campground pass by in a haze of wonder. The road rises on a bend, revealing the cool, green water of the river and the packs of brightly outfitted whitewater rafters floating its rapids.

The campground itself flanks the river and provides easy access to put in or take out a kayak, or simply to dangle your feet in its chilly waters. Most of the campsites themselves are well shaded by large, blue-green junipers. The trees are large enough that you can pitch a tent in the sandy clearings under their branches. Sage and scarlet paintbrush bloom alongside the sites. Each campsite has a picnic table and campfire ring. Along the main loop, there are two vault toilets; a third toilet can be found at the group area, which is actually just two double sites with four picnic tables, two campfire rings, and a trail connecting sites 1 and 2. Trash bins, with aluminum recycling bins, are situated near the toilets.

Rio Chama has 19 single sites, but not all of them are numbered—the three sites closest to the entrance may technically be considered overflow spots, but they also have picnic tables and fire rings. While RVs up to 20 feet can squeeze into some sites, not many drive the long gravel road to get here.

Several campsites at Rio Chama lead directly to the water.

KEY INFORMATION

LOCATION: FS 151, about 28 miles northwest of Abiquiú

CONTACT: Santa Fe National Forest, Coyote Ranger District, 575-638-5526, tinyurl.com/riochama

OPEN: Mid-April–late October

SITES: 19, including 2 double sites

EACH SITE HAS: Picnic table, fire ring

WHEELCHAIR ACCESS: None

ASSIGNMENT: First-come, first-served; no reservations

REGISTRATION: Not required

AMENITIES: Vault toilets but no potable water or electricity

PARKING: At sites

FEE: Free

ELEVATION: 6,488'

RESTRICTIONS

PETS: Permitted on leash

QUIET HOURS: 10 p.m.–6 a.m.

FIRES: In fire rings only

ALCOHOL: Permitted

OTHER: 14-day stay limit; no ATVs; no public nudity

Sites 2, 4, 6, and 8 all sit on the bank above the river. Site 4 even has steps that lead down to the water (the others have paths). Site 10 also appears to have river access; you must take a path through a marshy area thick with salt cedar. Sites 2, 4, 8, and 11 look the most spacious if you are traveling with a larger group. I stayed at sites 8 and 10, with eight people camping comfortably.

All of the sites are free and first-come, first-served, so plan to arrive early to claim a preferred site. When I've been here in May and July, the campground has only been half full, but the U.S. Forest Service reports heavy usage. If you happen to come and the campground is full, there is also dispersed camping at Oak Grove and Whirlpool, both also on Forest Service Road 151; some sites are on the riverbank.

FS 151 has frequent usage from commercial rafting and kayaking outfitters. They predominantly head to the day-use take-out area, Big Eddy. For being a gravel road with some washboard, the road is in good shape, but the Forest Service doesn't recommend driving it while its wet, so take care during monsoon season.

In addition to fun on the river and nearby hikes, there's plenty to fill your days along the Rio Chama. You can visit Georgia O'Keeffe's home, Ghost Ranch, which has hiking trails, a labyrinth, museums, and a summer outdoor swimming pool (open only in afternoons to day-use visitors). The trails lead you through canyons and atop ridges that appear to be straight out of one of O'Keeffe's paintings. In 1942, O'Keeffe wrote to the painter Arthur Dove, "I wish you could see what I see out the window—the earth pink and yellow cliffs to the north—the full pale moon about to go down in an early morning lavender sky . . . pink and purple hills in front and the scrubby fine dull green cedars—and a feeling of much space—it is a very beautiful world." Her ashes were scattered atop Cerro Pedernal, the bluish butte you can see in the distance, south of the lake. For a $5 fee to help maintain the facilities and trails, you can also check out a small paleontology museum that has *Coelophysis* fossils—about 1,000 specimens of this dinosaur have been unearthed near Ghost Ranch.

If you continue down FS 151, it dead-ends at the Benedictine Abbey of Christ in the Desert. The monks there run their own brewery, Abbey Brewing Company, founded in a 1,300-year-old tradition of hospitality that includes "liquid bread." In late August, you can help the brothers harvest hops from their experimental hop yard, which includes several varieties native to northern New Mexico.

The closest town with services is Abiquiú, about 28 miles southeast. The general store there, Bode's, has serviced "travelers, hunters, pilgrims, stray artists, and bandits since 1893." In addition to filling your car up with gasoline, Bode's also has a restaurant and a general store with everything from camping gear to piñon–oshá salve (a natural antiseptic ointment).

Rio Chama Campground

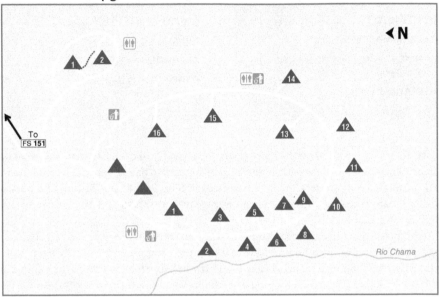

GETTING THERE

From Española, take US 84 West toward Chama. Continue for 38 miles; then, past Ghost Ranch, turn left (west) onto FS 151. After 12 miles, the campground will be on the left. Note that FS 151 may be impassable when wet.

GPS COORDINATES: N36° 21.339' W106° 40.398'

20

⛺ Rio de las Vacas Campground

Beauty ★★★★★ Privacy ★★★ Spaciousness ★★★★ Quiet ★★★★ Security ★★★★★ Cleanliness ★★★★

In late spring, Rio de las Vacas's waters swell with snowmelt; in the summer, you can fish for rainbow, brown, or Rio Grande cutthroat trout.

Rio de las Vacas begins at a spring in the San Pedro Parks Wilderness, flows through tall ponderosa pines, spruce and fir trees, and past the campground of the same name. It eventually converges with Rio Cebolla at Porter Landing to form the Rio Guadalupe. This river and its watershed have benefited from several wetlands action plans to plant Gooding's willows, stabilize the banks, improve wildlife and fish habitat, and educate about the health of the river.

In late spring, Rio de las Vacas's waters swell with snowmelt; in the summer, you can fish for rainbow, brown, or Rio Grande cutthroat trout. It has been reported that the fish will swim right up to any fly that lands on the water and take a bite. Even if you'd rather not tie and cast flies, you'll still find Rio de las Vacas a charming retreat. Rio de las Vacas has a little less of the traffic that the campgrounds outside of Jemez Springs get, even though it's only 2 hours from Albuquerque.

The 15 sites are spread along a small loop, with plenty of space between each one. The campground has two vault toilets (near the entrance and by site 8) and several trash bins dispersed throughout. You'll want to make sure to use these bins and to stow your food away at night in case raccoons stage a raid.

Sites 1–4 all lie streamside, so you can listen to the water as you turn in for the night or have easy access to the banks right from your campsite. Because the river is atop a granite

Snowmelt feeds the Rio de las Vacas in the late spring.

KEY INFORMATION

LOCATION: NM 126, 12 miles east of Cuba

CONTACT: Santa Fe National Forest, Cuba Ranger District, 575-289-3264, tinyurl.com/riodelasvacas

OPEN: May 15–September 30

SITES: 15

EACH SITE HAS: Picnic table, fire ring

WHEELCHAIR ACCESS: Accessible toilets

ASSIGNMENT: First-come, first-served only September 15–30; otherwise by reservation (877-444-6777, recreation.gov/camping/campgrounds/251437)

REGISTRATION: On-site or online

AMENITIES: Vault toilets, potable water

PARKING: At sites

FEE: $10/night ($5 with Interagency Pass)

ELEVATION: 8,252'

RESTRICTIONS

PETS: Permitted on leash

QUIET HOURS: 10 p.m.–6 a.m.

FIRES: In fire rings only

ALCOHOL: Allowed at campsites

OTHER: No ATVs; maximum 8 people/site. Trailers are limited to 16' in length; RVs, 30'. Do not collect artifacts.

bedrock, it's prone to flash flows during summer monsoons; however, these campsites are situated on a little hill above the water. These sites are all well shaded by pines, which is good for late sleepers but may mean you'll need to plan extra drying time for your tent during monsoon season. Site 4 seems particularly nice; it sits atop a hill on a little spur set back from the loop, which turns just before the site. These popular sites are in high demand; you'll need to arrive early to snag one.

The loop turns past pleasant site 5 and up the small hill. Sites 8, 9, and 10 have good views but are more exposed. They have little tree cover and little privacy, but they do have access to a fair-size meadow that is just waiting for a pick-up soccer game or some kids with a Frisbee. Also on this side of the loop, site 15 feels as though it's a little too close to the highway; luckily there isn't much traffic after sunset.

Along the river, thickets of willow grow; they fill with songbirds seasonally. Children of all ages enjoy playing in the river, scrambling over slick boulders, or strolling on the banks. Many locals also fish and play here; there is a day-use parking area just across the street from the campground's entrance. When I visited, one angler was headed home for the day, walking with his reel along the

Ponderosa pines tower over many of the sites at Rio de las Vacas Campground.

shoulder of the highway; a couple was out for a stroll, also on the shoulder; and two families with small children were playing under the bridge. Take care while you're driving to and from the campground and watch for these pedestrians.

In addition to people, ranging cattle (as you might have guessed from the name of the river) might pop up on the road from time to time. There is a cattle guard to keep them out of camp, though. This river and its watershed are also home to a variety of wildlife: beavers, the Mexican spotted owl, the New Mexico jumping mouse, and the Northern goshawk are just a few of the creatures you might spy while staying here. The nearby San Pedro Parks Wilderness has over 41,000 acres of forest to enjoy. Named for the meadows, or "parks," that break up the alpine forest, the wilderness has more than 30 miles of trails on gentle terrain—perfect for a mellow hike.

Cuba, only 12 miles away, will have most of what you need in the form of extra groceries and gas. From tableside guacamole to short-order burritos that taste homemade, the restaurants in Cuba will delight your taste buds and satisfy your cravings.

Rio de las Vacas Campground

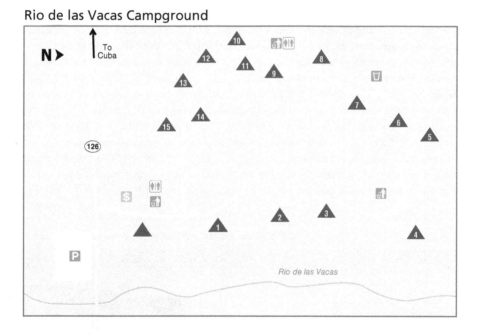

GETTING THERE

From US 550 in Cuba, turn east onto NM 126 at the visitor information center. After 12 miles, the campground will be on your left.

GPS COORDINATES: N35° 59.802' W106° 48.456'

21

⛺ Río Grande del Norte National Monument: ORILLA VERDE CAMPGROUNDS

Río Pueblo Campground Beauty ★★★★★ Privacy ★★★★ Spaciousness ★★★★★ Quiet ★★★ Security ★★★ Cleanliness ★★★★

All Other Campgrounds Beauty ★★★★ Privacy ★★★ Spaciousness ★★★ Quiet ★★★ Security ★★★★ Cleanliness ★★★★

Orilla Verde Recreation Area is a water enthusiast's dream: here, the Rio Grande flows gently, with occasional small rapids, and plenty of opportunity to spend the day floating the 7 miles between Taos Junction and Pilar.

Among the paddleboarders and whitewater rafters, families in inner tubes float down the Rio Grande. As we drove along the adjacent road, we could see a pair of boys strolling through the middle of the river, the water there only knee-deep and so calm that they hardly seemed to notice the kayakers and rafters on either side of them. Orilla Verde Recreation Area is a water enthusiast's dream: here, the Rio Grande flows gently, with occasional small rapids, and plenty of opportunity to spend the day floating the 7 miles between Taos Junction and Pilar.

Orilla Verde forms part of the Río Grande National Monument; Wild Rivers Recreation Area, to the north, is also part of the monument and also has camping (see next profile) but doesn't have the same water-recreation opportunities. This national monument was created as part of the Wild and Scenic Rivers Act of 1968; in 2019, it gained over 20,000 additional acres when the Cerro del Yuta Wilderness and the Rio Antonio Wilderness were added.

As you turn into the monument, you'll pass a small community, Pilar, with several art studios. The first campground shares this name. Pilar Campground has nine RV sites with electricity and water and three tent sites with shade structures, picnic tables, pedestal grills,

On a hot summer day, you can float—or often wade—down the river at the Orilla Verde Campgrounds.

KEY INFORMATION

LOCATION: Off NM 68 just north of the Rio Grand Gorge Visitor Center, Pilar, NM 87553

CONTACT: Bureau of Land Management, Taos Field Office, 575-758-8851, blm.gov /visit/orilla-verde-recreation-area

OPEN: Year-round

SITES: 7 campgrounds with 47 sites

EACH SITE HAS: Picnic table, fire ring

WHEELCHAIR ACCESS: Accessible parking; some accessible sites (see campground description)

ASSIGNMENT: First-come, first-served; no reservations

REGISTRATION: Self-register on-site

AMENITIES: Visitor center; several campgrounds have water, pay showers, small boat ramps

PARKING: At sites

FEE: $7/night nonelectric, $15/night electric

ELEVATION: 7,802'

RESTRICTIONS

PETS: Permitted on leash

QUIET HOURS: 10 p.m.–6 a.m.

FIRES: In fire rings only

ALCOHOL: Permitted

OTHER: 14-day stay limit; maximum 2 vehicles and 8 people/site; checkout is 10 a.m.; do not remove or disturb any artifacts

and campfire rings. Set back on a little hill, the only privacy these sites have is from the tall chamisa that obscures them from their associated parking spots. You can pick up La Senda del Medio Trail, which takes you off the road to Petaca Campground.

Rio Bravo Campground is another RV-friendly area (it has four RV sites); the restrooms here also have pay showers. Here's where you'll find the camp host for this stretch. On the river side of the road, with plenty of shade from large cottonwoods, this bustling campground has quite a few nice spaces. Seven campsites on the outer loop are all tent spaces, with gravel tent pads. By site 8, there's a group day-use shelter with several picnic tables. The parking area by site 4 includes an accessible van-parking space.

Arroyo Hondo Campground has five campsites, all tent sites. This campground doesn't have water, but it does have a vault toilet and trash receptacles, including recycling. Site 3 appears to be more spacious and to have a path directly to the river. Unfortunately, Arroyo Hondo doesn't have much shade, so you may want to pack your own shade structure.

Lone Juniper Campground has four sites, no water, two vault toilets, and a boat ramp. Sites 1 and 2 appeared to be accessible. While Lone Juniper has more cottonwoods and more shade, it's a very busy small campground. The boat ramp chokes the one-way road with vehicles putting in and taking out rafts.

Petaca Campground was closed for renovations when I visited, but it looked like they were keeping the established cottonwoods. Previously it had five campsites, water, and a vault toilet.

Taos Junction Campground sits across the river, accessible by bridge, and has four campsites and a group shelter. The toilet has running water; beside it, the camp host has created a "Lost and Found Garden." Discarded or forgotten shoes have become planters for creeping succulents; windbreakers and hats stand as scarecrows. Each site has an adobe-looking shade structure; they overlook the river below.

Rio Pueblo Campground, at the end of the line and back several yards from the river, has less traffic and the most spacious and private sites. Even though this campground is listed as primitive, the six sites are numbered, have picnic tables and campfire rings, and share a camp host and vault toilet. Sites 1 and 3 are ideal tent-camping locations—wilder and surrounded by juniper for privacy and shade.

The Friends of the Río Grande del Norte group has planted hundreds of trees to restore some of the riparian forests along the river. Volunteers have spotted river otters playing along the banks and bighorn sheep climbing the cliffs. You might also encounter mariposa lilies, cliff fendler bushes, and, of course, prickly pear blooming in several colors. In late summer, bushy sunflowers nod along the road.

As you drive among the campgrounds, watch out for people walking along the road with inner tubes in hand—the shoulder is narrow. From May 1 through October, the visitor center is open daily, 8:30 a.m.–4:30 p.m.; winter hours are 10 a.m.–2 p.m. In addition to a selection of books that make for good campfire reading, the visitor center sells firewood. The parking lot has a steady stream of rafting company vans picking up and dropping off whitewater adventurers.

Río Grande del Norte National Monument: Orilla Verde Campgrounds

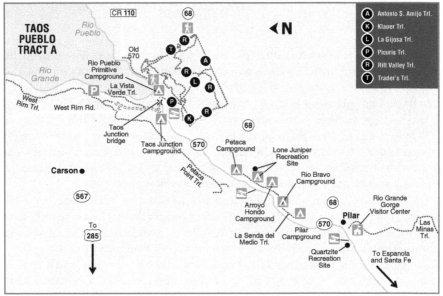

GETTING THERE

From Taos, drive north on US 64 West; in 4.1 miles, at the split with NM 522, bear left (west) to continue on US 64. In 8.7 miles, after you cross the Rio Grande Gorge Bridge, turn left (south) onto West Rim Road (Taos County Road CB-115). In 8.2 miles, continue south, now on NM 567. In 2.7 miles, after you cross the Taos Junction Bridge, the road bears right (southwest) and becomes NM 570. In 4.2 miles, Taos Junction Campground will be on your left.

For a less scenic approach, take NM 68 South from Taos 16.5 miles, and turn right (north) onto NM 570 at Pilar. In 1.2 miles, the campground will be on your right.

GPS COORDINATES: N36° 17.103' W105° 47.219'

22

⛺ Río Grande del Norte National Monument: WILD RIVERS CAMPGROUNDS

Beauty ★★★★★ Privacy ★★★★★ Spaciousness ★★★★★ Quiet ★★★★★ Security ★★★★ Cleanliness ★★★★★

In every bend of the bank, every riffle and rapid, every grain of sand on its shores, there is the story of the river, wild and beautiful.

Scattered with sagebrush and chamisa, the Taos Plateau is so wide and flat that you almost don't see the dark furrow of the Rio Grande Gorge until you're standing at its rim. Peering into the chasm, you'll spy basalt some 3–5 million years old in the form of black boulders and tall columns, some full of holes from gas pockets, intermixed with baked red earth from the heat of the initial lava flow. At the bottom flows the Rio Grande on its 1,885-mile-long journey to the Gulf of Mexico. In every bend of the bank, every riffle and rapid, in every grain of sand on its shores, there is the story of the river, wild and beautiful.

The Wild and Scenic Rivers Act of 1968 deemed this section of the Rio Grande, from the Colorado state line downstream to NM 96, protected due to its "outstandingly remarkable scenic, recreation, geologic, fish and wildlife, historic, and cultural" values. Along with the lower 4 miles of the Red River, this act protects the river in a free-flowing, wild state for future generations. Along the rim of the gorges, five small, separate campgrounds give you the choice of watching the sunset over the Rio Grande Gorge or the sunrise over the Red River. The campsites atop the plateau sit among piñon, juniper, and sagebrush, where it's grassy and arid. Many of these sites are close to the edge, which may make those with a fear of heights uncomfortable. Or you can set up at one of 16 primitive sites by hiking down to the trail

From the Rinconada Trail, you can stand near the edge of the gorge and applaud the magnficent New Mexican sunsets.

KEY INFORMATION

LOCATION: 1120 Cerro Road, Cerro, NM 87519

CONTACT: Bureau of Land Management, Taos Field Office, 575-758-8851 (call to reserve a group picnic shelter); Wild Rivers Visitor Center, 575-586-1150, blm.gov/visit /wild-rivers-recreation-area

OPEN: Year-round

SITES: 5 campgrounds with 40 sites, including 2 group shelters for up to 30 picnicking guests

EACH SITE HAS: Shade shelter over picnic table, pedestal grill, fire ring

WHEELCHAIR ACCESS: Accessible parking at all campgrounds, toilets, group shelters

ASSIGNMENT: First-come, first-served; no reservations except for group shelters

REGISTRATION: Self-register at any pay station near developed camping, picnic, and trailhead areas

AMENITIES: Vault toilets, potable water, visitor center

PARKING: Near sites, overnight parking lot for backpackers

FEE: $7/night ($3.50 with Interagency Pass); $5/night for river campsites; $30/day or $40/night for group shelters

ELEVATION: 7,553'

RESTRICTIONS

PETS: Permitted on leash except on Big Arsenic Trail or in freshwater springs

QUIET HOURS: 10 p.m.–6 a.m.

FIRES: In fire rings only

ALCOHOL: Permitted

OTHER: 14-day stay limit; maximum 2 vehicles and 8 people/site; no gathering firewood; no fireworks or firearms use; no horses; no public nudity; no bathing in water spigots; no motor-vehicle free play

near the river, shaded by towering ponderosa pines, wandering through dense gooseberry and riparian vegetation, and across cool springs.

As you enter, the first campground you'll come across is Big Arsenic, which has a vault toilet, water, and six sites. At all of the campsites on the top, there are shade structures over picnic tables, pedestal grills, and large campfire rings with grills. From the day-use parking lot here, the Big Arsenic Springs Trail drops 680 feet down to the river, following a mile-long switchback. Along the way, self-guided interpretive trail markers describe some of the local flora. Past the spring are more campsites, each with a shelter, a picnic table, and a stone fire pit. If you walk upstream, past the vault toilet, keep your eye out for petroglyphs on the basalt boulders.

Little Arsenic Campground has six sheltered sites, water, and a vault toilet. At the two Arsenic campgrounds and Montoso Campground, the campsites are set far enough apart that you forget other campers are there until a bright-orange flap of nylon surprises you through the trees, or you hear a sneeze 20 yards to the right. The trail here is 1 mile to the bottom, with a 760-foot elevation change. Horses are permitted on this trail. More backpacking campsites are scattered along the river.

Montoso Campground has four sites, water, and a vault toilet at the shared parking lot. The northernmost site has a labyrinth made of collected stones. According to the staff, the stones are periodically displaced and the labyrinth disassembled, but it always seems to get remade. Here, as with the other campgrounds, there is access to the Rinconada Loop Trail, which is an easy, flat, 6.1-mile loop connecting all of the campgrounds. Don't be surprised to see the staff biking it to collect camp fees.

La Junta ("The Meeting or Joining") Campground overlooks the confluence of the Rio Grande, rolling from the San Juan Mountains of Southern Colorado, and the Red River, flowing from the Sangre del Cristo Mountains. La Junta is both the widest and deepest spot of the Rio Grande Gorge—here it's 0.75 mile wide and drops 800 feet. The campground here has an accessible group shelter, a concession stand (not staffed), potable water, and three campsites with shelters. The path to the overlook is paved for wheelchairs. A difficult (due to steepness) 1.2-mile trail takes you to the bottom—if your quads can handle it. This trail also has several backpacking campsites.

The camp host can be found at El Aguaje (pronounced "ah-wah-hay") Campground, which is on the Red River side. Along with seven campsites, there is also a group day-use shelter that accommodates up to 30 people for picnicking. While El Aguaje may have the most pop-ups, van campers, and small RVs, it offers only water and a toilet, as there are no RV hookups in the whole monument. The trail here is 0.7 mile to Red River and only loses 500 feet in elevation on its way to the water and the campsites below.

In addition to the trails that leave from the campgrounds, the Guadalupe Mountain Trail offers spectacular views of the volcanic plateau and the gorge. This trail takes off from an interior road between Chiflo Trail and Bear Crossing Trail. Be prepared for a difficult, steep climb—in the 2.1 miles to the top, you'll climb 1,000 feet in elevation.

Depending on the availability of staff, the visitor center is open Thursday–Sunday, Memorial Day–Labor Day. In addition to an informative display about the area, they sell hats and sunblock, field guides, firewood ($3 a bundle), and ice ($2 a bag).

Río Grande del Norte National Monument: Wild Rivers Campgrounds

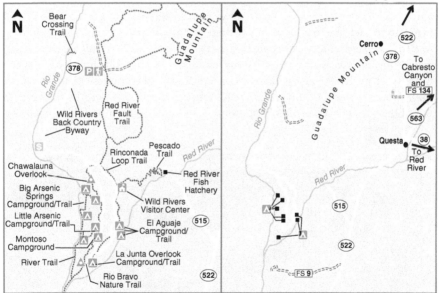

GETTING THERE

From Taos, drive north on US 64 West; in 4.1 miles, at the split with NM 522, bear right (northeast) to continue on NM 522. In 23.7 miles, or about 3 miles past the stoplight in Questa, turn left (west, then north) onto NM 387, which becomes NM 378. Follow the signs for Wild Rivers Recreation Area; the visitor center is about 12 miles past the turnoff.

GPS COORDINATES: N36° 40.848' W105° 40.382'

23

⛺ San Antonio Campground

Beauty ★★★ Privacy ★ Spaciousness ★★ Quiet ★★ Security ★★★ Cleanliness ★★★

A paved walk follows the water; trodden paths lead to its sylvan banks for fishing access or for children to play in.

On the road to Fenton Lake, there's a hidden oasis tucked among the ponderosa pines. Named for the San Antonio Creek, which meanders alongside the southern edge of the campground, San Antonio Campground was rebuilt in 2010 and still feels brand-new. A paved walk follows the water; trodden paths lead to its sylvan banks for fishing access or for children to play in.

San Antonio, like the other Jemez campgrounds, fills up fast nearly every day, so you'll need to plan early to pick the best sites—when I visited, two family reunions had nearly the whole campground booked. You may be able to walk in a month before and a month after the campground is officially open (that is, early May and October); contact the Jemez Ranger District for details.

Six campsites have water and electrical hookups, 11 are standard nonelectric sites, and 3 sites are both tent-only and nonelectric. Unfortunately, the four designated tent sites (26–29) are squeezed together in a tight row between a fenced meadow and a steep hill. A footpath runs from their parking lot to the farthest site and dead-ends. There's so little space, it's hard to imagine jamming six people into a site. What's more, the sites are hit hard by the afternoon sun and have a view of La Cueva's cabins and corrals. If you pick a site nearer to the water (such as site 3), you can listen to the creek instead of the well-trafficked highway.

San Antonio is one of the most accessible campgrounds I've visited. The website claims that all of the sites are ADA-compliant, but I would question that for the tent-only sites.

Bordering a meadow, the dedicated tent sites at San Antonio Campground form a tidy row.

KEY INFORMATION

ADDRESS: NM 126, Jemez Springs, NM 87025

CONTACT: Santa Fe National Forest, Jemez Ranger District, 575-829-3535, tinyurl.com/sanantoniocampground

OPEN: Mid-May–mid-September

SITES: 20, plus a group area with 9 walk-in sites

EACH SITE HAS: Picnic table, fire ring with grill, and lantern pole. Some sites have tent pads; some have pedestal grills.

WHEELCHAIR ACCESS: Accessible fishing, paved walk, restrooms, and all campsites

ASSIGNMENT: By reservation only mid-May–September (877-444-6777, recreation.gov /camping/campgrounds/233390); first-come, first-served sites sometimes available in the off-season

REGISTRATION: Check in with camp host upon arrival

AMENITIES: Vault toilets, drinking water, and recycle bins

PARKING: At sites except sites 26–29, which share a small parking lot

FEE: $10/per night

ELEVATION: 7,802'

RESTRICTIONS

PETS: Permitted on leash

QUIET HOURS: 10 p.m.–6 a.m.

FIRES: In fire rings only

ALCOHOL: Permitted

OTHER: 14-day stay limit; maximum 2 vehicles/ site; maximum 10 people/standard site or 6 people/tent-only site; check-in at 3 p.m., checkout at 2 p.m. Dead and downed wood in the forest can be picked up for firewood. No shooting firearms, BB guns, sling shots, wrist rockets, or archery bows. Cell reception is poor here.

However, the paved walk does have gravel outcrops to provide fishing areas for those in wheelchairs. The group site here would be great to rent for an event—unlike many others, which seem to be just a field, vault toilet, and shared pavilion.

San Antonio has nine walk-in campsites, each with its own picnic table and fire ring. Plus, it has the requisite pavilion, which can accommodate up to 100 people. The U.S. Forest Service has designated San Antonio as a reduced-impact and recycle campground, meaning they encourage you to recycle using the bins on-site, pack out your trash, and bring in your own potable water if you can. On-site potable water is available from spigots near each of the toilets, but there may be restrictions in effect. Additionally, the rangers request that you not cut live vegetation, set up tents in the grass, or remove firewood from the campground (it may spread beetles and other pests from one part of the forest to another).

To get to the San Antonio Hot Springs, turn left (west) on NM 126 (toward Fenton Lake), then right (north) on Forest Service Road 376 (near mile marker 35). The road is unpaved and rough. The parking area will be on you right, about 5 miles down the road. From there, all that separates you from the most beautiful of the Jemez hot springs is a short, steep hike. The gate to FS 376 is locked from mid-December to June 1, making it a 10-mile round trip hike along the closed road. Spence Hot Springs are also popular and easier to approach. Their sandy bottoms, 106°F mineral water, and beautiful views of the mountains make for a lovely soak any time of year. The parking lot for Spence is 7 miles north of Jemez Springs on the east side of NM 4. If the parking lot is full, that means the springs are too. For the most solitude, visit in the early morning.

A word of warning about hot springs: while it's extremely rare, a parasitic amoeba called *Naegleria fowleri,* known to cause a disease called primary amoebic meningoencephalitis, also happens to enjoy the warm waters of hot springs. While there have been only 145 cases of this disease documented since 1962—and only 1 case in New Mexico—it's best to keep the water from getting in your nose. Don't splash or submerge yourself entirely, and you should be fine. Also, please be aware that nudity is common at hot springs.

If you find yourself in need of toiletries and such, La Cueva is in view of the campground and would be an easy walk from the campground, but it may be dangerous if you walk on the road. There you'll find a bait-and-tackle general store, a family-run restaurant, and outdoor recreation rentals. For dinner, a massage, or a soak in a managed hot spring, you'll have to return to Jemez Springs. The nearest gas stations are in Jemez Pueblo, about 23 miles south, and Los Alamos, 31 miles east.

San Antonio Campground

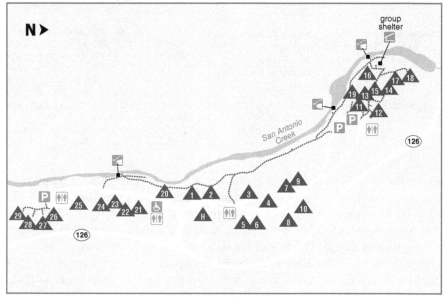

GETTING THERE

From Jemez Springs, drive 9 miles north on NM 4 and turn left (northwest) onto NM 126 in La Cueva. The campground is 2 miles farther, on the left.

GPS COORDINATES: N35° 53.200' W106° 38.766'

24

Santa Barbara Campground

Beauty ★★★★★ Privacy ★★★ Spaciousness ★★★★ Quiet ★★★★ Security ★★★ Cleanliness ★★★★★

A lovely view of the mountains—lush, green, and forested, flecked with blue shadows— will keep you company as you linger at your picnic table.

On cool summer days, fog mingles with smoke from early-morning campfires; together they drift through the firs and spruces of this canyon campground, filtering the sun's first rays. Bordered by ridges on either side, Santa Barbara Campground greets sunrise late, keeping mornings cool and giving you more time to enjoy that cup of coffee before hiking into the woods on one of the trails that start here. A lovely view of the mountains—lush, green, and forested, flecked with blue shadows—will keep you company as you linger at your picnic table.

Santa Barbara's single loop is structured so that sites 3–6 sit atop a slight ridge; this offset elevation does the trick to help these sites feel more private and separated from the rest of the loop below. Site 7 seems very spacious, nicely situated on the outside of the loop with access to the river. This site, however, is also right by the trailhead—so be prepared for a steady stream of hikers and fishermen saying hello as they pass. Sites 7–21 back up to Rio Santa Barbara, and several access points break the fence and lead to the river. Sites 19–21 are the most RV-friendly sites, but they are incredibly spacious compared with other campgrounds' RV areas. Site 20 practically has a field unto itself.

The trail from Santa Barbara Campground leads to the boundary of two national forests.

KEY INFORMATION

LOCATION: FS 116, 7 miles south of Peñasco

CONTACT: Carson National Forest,
Camino Real Ranger District, 575-587-2255,
tinyurl.com/santabarbaracampground;
Scenic Canyons (concessionaire),
435-245-6521, seniccanyons.com

OPEN: Mid-May–last weekend of September

SITES: 21

EACH SITE HAS: Picnic table, fire ring,
and pedestal grill

WHEELCHAIR ACCESS: Sites 11 and 12;
accessible parking

ASSIGNMENT: First-come, first-served and
by reservation (877-444-6777, recreation
.gov/camping/campgrounds/273360)

REGISTRATION: Self-register on-site or online

AMENITIES: Two vault toilets, potable water

PARKING: At sites

FEE: $17/single ($8.50 with Interagency Pass),
$32/double, $47/triple, $62/group;
$5/additional vehicle

ELEVATION: 8.878'

RESTRICTIONS

PETS: Permitted on leash

QUIET HOURS: 10 p.m.–6 a.m.

FIRES: In fire rings only

ALCOHOL: Permitted at sites

OTHER: 14-day stay limit; no ATVs; no saddle,
pack, or draft animals; no shooting;
no trailhead parking in campground

This campground has only two vault toilets, but they never feel far from the campsites. The one on the river side of the loop has paved sidewalks to sites 11 and 12, the two wheelchair-accessible spots that flank the vault toilet. These two sites are also paved and flat to make them more accessible. Near each toilet, you will also find a dumpster. Water spigots are more plentiful and spaced throughout the loop.

Santa Barbara has two group sites, 1 and 18, and one triple site (2), but these sites don't seem particularly spacious for a group, especially if you have a family of tent campers. If you're planning on camping with a group, you might do better to occupy two adjacent sites—sites 4 and 5, for example, would be particularly nice as a joint site. *Note:* There is currently no site numbered 17.

In late-summer afternoons, steely gray clouds gather on the horizon, the temperature drops, and after hours of threatening to rain, the monsoon finally unleashes its torrent. I camped here during a 4-hour downpour—the camp host later reported 1.35 inches of rain—and my tent stayed dry on the inside. The loop's slight ridge, combined with the gentle slope of the higher campsites, helps ensure that most of the rain finds its way into the Rio Santa Barbara. However, the late appearance of sunshine in the canyon, coupled with the shade, delayed my morning departure while I waited for my wet tent to dry on the outside.

Because the campground sits at such a high altitude, nestled in the woods, it stays quite cool most of the day and can be cold at night, so pack warm layers and remember the firewood if there aren't any forest-wide fire restrictions. Just outside the campground, hikers leave their cars in the trailhead parking before heading into the wilderness to Jicarita Peak Ridge. Fishermen grab their reels to cast in the Rio Santa Barbara, ready to hook rainbow and brown trout near the campground and, closer to the confluence, to catch and release Rio Grande cutthroat trout and Gila trout. At the nearby equestrian parking, horsepackers saddle up for the popular ride into Pecos Wilderness.

From the campground, you can start on a couple of popular trails. West Fork Trail 25 climbs the canyon, gaining 3,000 feet to the Santa Barbara Divide (12,000'). To the northeast, you'll have a great view of Chimayosos Peak. Before the final ascent, you'll also see No Fish Lake (11,600'), so named because it freezes solid in winter. The Santa Barbara Divide also marks the boundary between Carson and Santa Fe National Forests. This trail continues to Trail 251 and Truchas Lakes. Dense fog can sometimes make hiking here difficult or impossible—wait for a break in the weather before continuing.

Peñasco is the closest town with brunch options and conveniences, but your best bet for gas will be in Pojoaque or Las Vegas. The popular Sugar Nymphs Bistro in Peñasco can have an hour wait on the weekends due to sightseers cruising the High Road to Taos. Down the road, you'll find another café, more hiking, another campground (Comales, 15 miles east on NM 75), and Sipapu Ski & Summer Resort.

Santa Barbara Campground

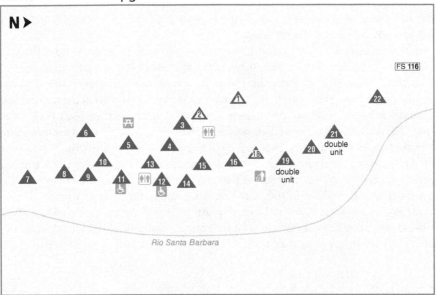

GETTING THERE

From the intersection of NM 75 and NM 73 in Peñasco, head southeast on NM 73 for 1.7 miles; at the fork, turn right (southeast) onto Santa Barbara Road, which becomes NM 73 and then Forest Service Road 116. After about 6 miles, the road dead-ends at the campground.

GPS COORDINATES: N36° 05.319' W105° 36.658'

25

⛺ Sugarite Canyon State Park:
LAKE ALICE AND SODA POCKET CAMPGROUNDS

Lake Alice Campground Beauty ★★★★★ Privacy ★★★ Spaciousness ★★★ Quiet ★★★★★
Security ★★★★★ Cleanliness ★★★★★

Soda Pocket Campground Beauty ★★★★★ Privacy ★★★★ Spaciousness ★★★★ Quiet ★★★★★
Security ★★★★★ Cleanliness ★★★★★

A daylong count found 637 butterflies of 38 different species here.

Just south of the Colorado state line, Sugarite Canyon State Park was once a coal-mining camp, where miners dug tunnels into the hillside coal seams. The name *Sugarite* (pronounced "shug-ur-eet") is believed to come from a Ute or Comanche word for a species of spotted bird that lives in the canyon or the Spanish word *chicorica*, which refers to the wild endive chicory (and is also the name of a creek to Lake Maloya). Since 1985, this beautiful canyon has been a state park and a top camping destination.

The first campground you'll come across is Lake Alice, directly across from the body of water with the same name. This campground, with water and electrical hookups, is better suited for RVs. You can reserve these sites online. Many have shelters; site 10 is accessible. The walk to the visitor center doesn't take long if you're hankering for a warm shower at the comfort station.

About a mile north of Lake Alice, there is a turnoff on the left for Soda Pocket Campground. The road climbs to the first-come, first-served campground. Ideal for tent campers, many sites have lots of greenery, and they are well spaced. Some come with shelters over the picnic tables, while others have shade provided by ponderosa pines. Some sites have bear boxes—bears are often seen in the state park, so you'll want to use the boxes provided or stow your food and toiletries in your car. There's no water at this campground.

Soda Pocket has great views of the canyon. At the top of the campground loop, you can hike the short (0.5-mile) Vista Grande Nature Trail for a panoramic view of the canyon and plains. A little ways down the road from Soda Pocket, the rangers host campfire programs.

Even in late winter, the hillsides in Sugarite Canyon pop with color.

KEY INFORMATION

LOCATION: 211 NM 526, Raton, NM 87740

CONTACT: Sugarite Canyon State Park, 575-445-5607, emnrd.state.nm.us/SPD /sugaritecanyonstatepark.html

OPEN: Lake Alice, year-round; Soda Pocket, May–October

SITES: Lake Alice, 16; Soda Pocket, 23

EACH SITE HAS: Picnic table, fire ring; some sites have shelters, pedestal grills, or bear boxes

WHEELCHAIR ACCESS: Site 10 at Lake Alice

ASSIGNMENT: By reservation (14) at Lake Alice (877-664-7787, newmexico.reserve america.com) until October 1, then they become first-come, first-served; first-come, first-served (23 sites) at Soda Pocket

REGISTRATION: Self-register on-site or online

AMENITIES: Comfort station with showers and flush toilets, vault toilets, group site, boat dock, visitor center

PARKING: At sites

FEE: $10/night nonelectric; $14/night electric; $10/additional vehicle

ELEVATION: 6,664'

RESTRICTIONS

PETS: Permitted on leash

QUIET HOURS: 10 p.m.–7 a.m.

FIRES: In fire rings and grills only

ALCOHOL: Allowed at sites; no glass containers

OTHER: Please pick up trash, including fishing line; 14-day stay limit; check-in at 4 p.m., checkout at 2 p.m.

You can reserve the Gambel Oak Group Area online. This group site can accommodate up to 7 vehicles, but each vehicle in addition to the reservation holder must pay $10. There are 8–10 tables, two bear boxes, a group barbecue grill, and adjacent vault toilets and trash cans. The Valve Tender's House is a historical building that has been renovated; the area around it has been developed into a primitive group picnic area. To reserve this group area, call ahead. It can fit about six vehicles.

Summers here are cool; the average high temperature in July is 78°F, dropping to 47°F at night. Inquire with the ranger about fire restrictions before trying to warm up with a campfire. Ponderosa pine, Gambel oak, and locust cover the hills; narrowleaf cottonwood and willow grow streamside. Mint and wild licorice grow in some of the meadows near riparian zones. According to the park rangers, Sugarite Canyon is teeming with wildlife: elk, mule deer, white-tailed deer, turkeys, bears, eagles, ospreys, various ducks and geese, and a wealth of songbirds call these woods home. You may even encounter a "Sugarite Road-block" when a rafter of wild turkeys crosses the road.

During the summer, the rangers host a butterfly festival with guided walks. One daylong count found 637 butterflies of 38 different species. The park also has honeybee hives. The canyon has several hiking trails to keep you walking and wandering throughout the park. From the visitor center, you can stroll along an interpretative trail that goes through the ruins of the old mining camp, which closed down in the 1940s. Deer Run Trail connects the campgrounds, while the other trails skirt Little Horse Mesa and the shores of Lake Maloya. You can find more information about hiking and recreation at the visitor center.

Part of the Opportunity Trail burned in the 2011 Track Fire; take precautions when hiking during high winds and rains, when burned trees may fall, and watch out for stump holes caused by burned tree roots. Bow hunting is permitted in season (April 15–May 10 and all of September and November); bring bright colors for you—and your dog—to wear while hiking.

In winter, Lake Maloya and Lake Alice open to ice fishing, once the ice grows thick enough to support even the hardiest of anglers. Rangers post frequent updates on the lake's suitability for this winter sport; call ahead for details. In winter, you may see bald eagles at the lakes. Of course, fishing in these two artificial lakes is also a great summer activity, as they're stocked with rainbow and brown trout. On the basalt cliffs, there are more than 40 established climbing routes. No bolting is allowed; these are mostly trad and top-roping climbs with a nice range of difficulty, from 5.8s to 5.12s, and lots of pockets. Across the border in Colorado, the park adjoins two state wildlife areas: Lake Dorothy and James M. John. There you'll find additional camping if you strike out at the park.

The visitor center has an interactive interpretive display about the history of Sugarite Canyon. You can purchase ice and water at the gift shop. You may be able to purchase firewood from the camp host. The closest services are in Raton, only 6 miles down the road.

Sugarite Canyon State Park: Lake Alice and Soda Pocket Campgrounds

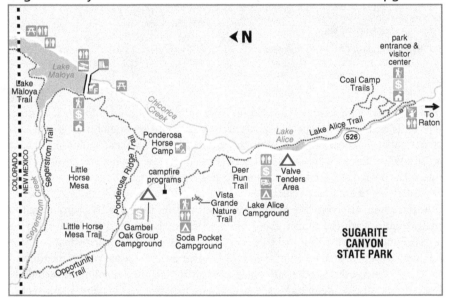

GETTING THERE

From I-25 in Raton, take Exit 452 and head east on NM 72. In 3.7 miles, bear left (northwest) at the fork onto NM 526, and drive 2 miles to the park entrance. Continue 3.1 miles farther on NM 526, and Lake Alice Campground will be on your left.

To reach Soda Pocket Campground, continue 1 mile north on NM 526, and turn left (west) onto Soda Pocket Road. In 1.7 miles, the campground entrance will be straight ahead.

GPS COORDINATES:
Lake Alice N36° 57.544′ W104° 23.180′
Soda Pocket N36° 58.480′ W104° 23.713′

26

Valle Vidal:
MCCRYSTAL AND CIMARRON CAMPGROUNDS

Beauty ★★★★★ Privacy ★★★★ Spaciousness ★★★★ Quiet ★★★★ Security ★★★★ Cleanliness ★★

During monsoon season, the grassy slopes of the valley pop with color from wildflowers: reds from paintbrush, penstemon, and skyrocket; purples from gentians, geranium, and iris; and yellow from cinquefoils and dandelions.

If you take the turns slowly on the gravel road through Cerrososo Canyon, peer into the clearings, and just beyond the young ponderosas, you might see a herd of elk. To bolster the population, one herd was purchased from Yellowstone National Park at $5 each in the 1950s—bison, wild turkeys, and Hereford cattle were introduced by the same rancher. Now there are about 2,500 elk, and there are special seasonal restrictions to ease their stress from human activity—including closure of the road from Costilla during calving season (April–June).

Donated by the Pennzoil Company in 1982, the Valle Vidal Unit of Carson National Forest is a treasure of pristine public wilderness in northern New Mexico. Ponderosa and bristlecone pines line grassy meadows. Sandstone breaks out of the hills here and there. As of 2019, Little Costilla and Comanche Creeks are eligible for Wild and Scenic Rivers designations, representing the "vestiges of primitive America." Comanche Point, at the confluence of the two creeks, is a remarkable geological formation, believed to have formed at the center of an impact crater—when an asteroid hit the volcanic rock, the pressure and

In Valle Vidal, you can alternate days of backcountry hikes with rest at Shuree Lakes.

KEY INFORMATION

LOCATION: McCrystal, FS 1950; Cimarron, FS 1910; both are about 36 miles east of Costilla

CONTACT: Carson National Forest, Questa Ranger District, 575-586-0520, tinyurl.com/mccrystalcampground, tinyurl.com/cimarroncampground

OPEN: Late May–late September

SITES: McCrystal, 60; Cimarron, 36

EACH SITE HAS: Picnic table, fire ring; many sites have corrals, string lines, and feeder boxes for horses

WHEELCHAIR ACCESS: McCrystal, sites 4 and 6; Cimarron, sites 3 and 17

ASSIGNMENT: First-come, first-served at McCrystal; some reservable sites at Cimarron (877-444-6777, recreation.gov/camping /campgrounds/233389)

REGISTRATION: Self-register on-site or online

AMENITIES: Vault toilets, troughs for horses (*note:* no human-potable water at McCrystal)

PARKING: At sites

FEE: McCrystal, $13/night; Cimarron, $20/ night single, $34/night double; $5/additional vehicle at both campgrounds

ELEVATION: McCrystal, 8,126'; Cimarron, 9,494'

RESTRICTIONS

PETS: Permitted on leash; watch your pets around horses

QUIET HOURS: 10 p.m.–8 a.m.

FIRES: In fire rings only

ALCOHOL: At campsites only

OTHER: 32' RV length limit

---

temperatures became so high that the rock instantly melted, forming new columns of rock after it cooled. While this lush mountain basin (*Valle Vidal* means "Valley of Life" in Spanish) is just north of the popular Red River, you'll find less of a crowd here.

During monsoon season, the grassy slopes of the valley pop with color from wildflowers: reds from paintbrush, penstemon, and skyrocket; purples from gentians, geranium, and iris; and yellow from cinquefoils and dandelions. In September, just before the campgrounds close, you can enjoy the stunning autumn beauty and listen to the elk bugling at night. In late spring and early fall, days can be cool and nights nippy; many campers build fires to warm up in the morning.

There are no defined trails through the meadows and timber of the valley, although you may find the occasional trail made by frequent use. These two campgrounds are remote, so make sure to stock up on water and gas in either Cimarron or Costilla if you're running low.

McCRYSTAL CAMPGROUND

This large campground has 60 sites nestled among young "blackjack" ponderosa pines. Six of the campsites are outfitted for horses, complete with corrals, string lines, and feeder boxes. The campground also has water troughs for the horses, but signs warn that the water is not meant for human consumption. At the end of the loop, near site 46, there is a large grill for group cooking.

Once the snow melts, crowds sometimes gather to look for shed antlers in the nearby meadows. When I visited, one camper proudly displayed her finds on the picnic table: a stack of three intact cow skulls. This campground may be filled with Scouts during the summer; if you'd rather avoid large groups of children, call ahead or plan on staying at Cimarron (see below). Although there is no on-site host here, security isn't an issue thanks to the concessionaire host just up the road at the other campground, as well as visits from rangers.

Near the entrance, an informative sign marks the start of a mile-long, self-guided interpretive trail. The markers enlighten campers about some of the history of the valley, including the logging towns of Ring and Ponil Park (which shipped wood to Cimarron and Raton on an old railroad) and one-time residents John and Annie McCrystal, for whom the campground is named.

Valle Vidal: McCrystal Campground

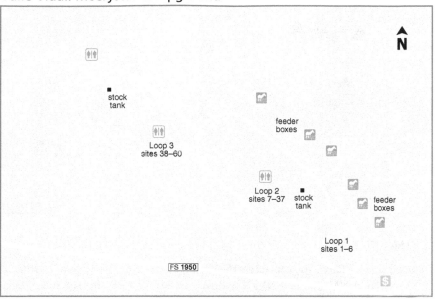

CIMARRON CAMPGROUND

The smaller of the two campgrounds, Cimarron Campground is a little more spread out than McCrystal; plus, it has more trees and a greater sense of privacy. And at 1,000 feet higher in elevation, it may make you feel winded (unless you've acclimated). An on-site host is ready to help you locate your reservation and give advice about fishing and roaming the hills.

Cimarron is divided into two loops, each with two pit toilets and a water spigot. Of the 36 sites, 9 are specifically for horses, 2 are double sites, and 25 are single sites. The two accessible sites here have gravel ramps and paths lined with boards.

Chipmunks are frequent visitors to all sites, sunning themselves on rocks and poking around for any food left unattended. Just outside the camp, a row of bear-proof trash cans secures waste and provides a reminder to be bear-aware while camping here.

Anglers might land a Rio Grande cutthroat trout in Comanche Creek and Rio Pueblo; make note of signs designating streams as special Red Chile Waters. From site 24, you can pick up a trail that, in a half mile, delivers you to Shuree Ponds. From July 1 to December 31, you can fish for rainbow trout in the large pond, and kids under 12 can try their luck in the smaller one.

On hot summer days, take care not to cast onto someone floating in an inner tube—nonmotorized watercraft are permitted on the small ponds.

Valle Vidal: Cimarron Campground

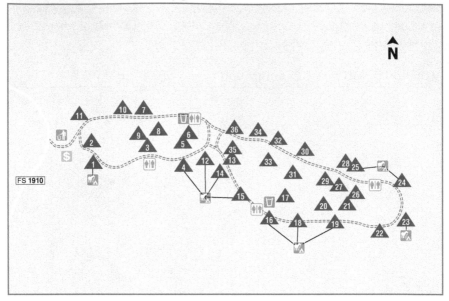

GETTING THERE

From July through March, you can access the campgrounds from the town of Costilla. From the intersection of NM 522 and NM 196, drive east on NM 196. In 14.8 miles, bear left at the fork to continue southeast on NM 196. In 3.8 miles, turn right (south) at a second fork across Costilla Creek to continue on this road; then, in 4.3 miles, bear left (southeast) at a third fork. In 3.8 miles, continue east as the road becomes Forest Service Road 1950. In 1.2 miles, turn right (southeast) at the fork onto FS 1910, and in 0.8 mile Cimarron Campground will be on your left. If you turn left at the previous fork, staying on FS 1950, McCrystal Campground is 9.1 miles farther on the left.

During elk-calving season (April–June), the gate at Costilla is locked. From the intersection of NM 204 and US 64 in Cimarron, drive east on US 64 for 3.4 miles; then turn left (north) onto FS 1950. After 30 miles, McCrystal Campground will be on your right. Cimarron Campground is an additional 9 miles west on FS 1950—at the junction with FS 1910, turn left and the campground will be a mile uphill.

Note: Gravel roads may require a four-wheel-drive vehicle during monsoon season.

GPS COORDINATES:
   McCrystal N36° 46.666′ W105° 06.755′
   Cimarron N36° 46.220′ W105° 12.296′

27

⛺ Villanueva State Park Campground

Beauty ★★★★★ Privacy ★★★★ Spaciousness ★★★ Quiet ★★★ Security ★★★★★ Cleanliness ★★★★

When the Pecos swells with snowmelt and flows high, campers come to canoe, kayak, and raft.

Yellow and red sandstone bluffs rise above the Pecos River, forming a picturesque backdrop to the park. Plenty of cottonwoods shade the banks of the river; farther up the hill, juniper and piñons create privacy between campsites. When the Pecos swells with snowmelt and flows high, campers come to canoe, kayak, and raft. From October to April, the river is stocked with rainbow trout; in the summer, catfish become the fare.

A sign at the entrance proudly proclaims Villanueva State Park as part of the Route of Conquistadores, noting that Francisco Vasquez Coronado (1540), Francisco "Chamuscado" Sánchez, Fray Agustín Rodriguez, Hernando Gallego (1581), and Antonio de Espejo and Castaño de Sosa (1592–93) all passed through. In addition to Pueblo occupation (700–1400 C.E.) as evidenced by archaeological finds, this area was also frequented by Comanche and Jicarilla Apache who hunted here. Originally called La Cuesta, Villanueva was settled in the 1820s as part of the San Miguel Del Vado Land Grant. The park was established in 1967, when land was donated to the state and additional parcels were purchased from local residents.

The campground is split into two distinct sections: you can camp by the river (25 sites) or atop the hill in El Cerro Campground (11 sites). The river spots remain open for camping year-round; several have stucco shade structures that look like adobe casitas tucked between hedges made from coyote willow by the river and juniper near the road. It's well shaded by

Stop to catch your breath at the lookout on Viewpoint Loop Trail.

KEY INFORMATION

LOCATION: 135 Dodge Dr., Villanueva, NM 87583

CONTACT: Villanueva State Park, 575-412-2957, emnrd.state.nm.us/SPD /villanuevastatepark.html

OPEN: River sites, year-round; El Cerro, April–November

SITES: 36

EACH SITE HAS: Picnic table, fire ring; many sites have stone shelters

WHEELCHAIR ACCESS: Accessible restrooms, site 14

ASSIGNMENT: First-come, first-served and by reservation (877-664-7787, newmexicostateparks.reserveamerica.com)

REGISTRATION: Self-register at entrance or online

AMENITIES: Visitor center, vault toilets, water, group shelter, playground, dump station, restrooms with showers, flush toilets, and sinks

PARKING: At sites

FEE: $10/night; $14/night with electric; $10/additional vehicle

ELEVATION: 5,785'

RESTRICTIONS

PETS: Permitted on leashes; please clean up after your pet

QUIET HOURS: 10 p.m.–7 a.m.

FIRES: In fire pits only

ALCOHOL: Permitted at sites

OTHER: Checkout at 2 p.m; no glass containers; no cutting wood. Summer gate closure 9 p.m.–7 a.m.; winter 7 p.m.–7 a.m. The ranger office/visitor center is open daily, 7 a.m.–4 p.m., May–September.

cottonwood, and most sites have soft sand to pitch your tent on. I would reserve site 19 in a heartbeat—wonderfully private and shaded thanks to the trees, with its own river access. Families would love site 22, since it sits just across from the playground and is spacious. Across from the ranger office/visitor center is a comfort station with flush toilets, sinks, and a shower. It's open 24 hours a day in the summer and from 7 a.m. to 3:30 p.m. in the winter. You can reserve the following sites: 6, 7, 9, and the group shelter all have electricity; 19, 21, and 22 are nonelectric. Site 14 is ADA-accessible and has electricity but cannot be reserved.

El Cerro Campground opens April 1 and stays open until the first snow, which has been in November the past few years. Many of these have stone shade structures over picnic tables, walls of juniper for privacy, and fire rings with grills. This hill has two distinct areas; sites 26–29 share a vault toilet, two spigots, and fantastic sunset views of the hills and valley below. Site 26 sits a little downslope from the others and would afford more privacy. The other seven, on the eastern side of the hill, share a vault toilet; not all of them have shade structures, and most have gravel areas for your tent. Site 36 has a good view of the sunrise, but it doesn't have much tent space. However, the stone structure might be big enough to scoot the picnic table to one side and pitch a small tent inside. Site 33 would be best avoided—it's right next to the road, and without a stone structure, it's exposed to constant sun, wind, and traffic.

Campers at Villanueva State Park evidently enjoy playing: in addition to the playground, there are poles set up for two volleyball nets. By the playground, two picnic tables are available for day use. Near the plumbed restrooms, there is also a foot washing station to rinse your feet after splashing around in the river. Near the bridge, the park has a great group shelter, with a large stone fireplace, several tables, and a stone building for shade.

Crossing the Pecos River on the bridge, you'll come to the trailhead for one of three hikes. The Viewpoint Loop Trail (2 miles) climbs the sandstone bluff and provides several great views of the village below, the farmland adjacent to the park, and the park itself. Some interpretive signs point out Spanish ruins—stone-walled corrals and pens for threshing wheat. The Spanish settlers drove horses in circles to trample sheaves of grain, then winnowed it by tossing it up in the air. At the top, a spur leads to three shade structures and more beautiful views. Deer and bobcat tracks mixed with hiking boot prints in the soft sand of the trail; a bear left his calling card in one of the structures. Another trail heads out from El Cerro Campground; about a mile total, this out-and-back leads to a vista on the opposite side of the river, then drops down to connect to a short riverbank trail.

Pecos is the closest town with services to the north; to the south, you can always stop at Clines Corners, with a 30,000-square-foot rest stop, gas station, and gift shop originally built in 1937.

Villanueva State Park Campground

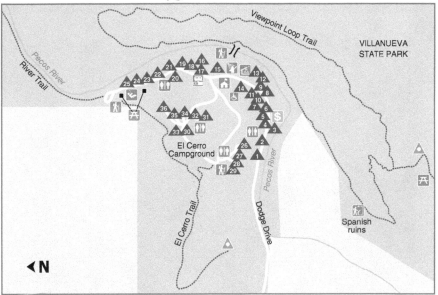

GETTING THERE

From Albuquerque, take I-40 East for 71 miles to Exit 230 (NM 3 North). Take NM 3 North about 20 miles to the town of Villanueva, following the signs for the state park. Turn right (east) onto County Road B28E/County Road B29E, and in 0.4 mile continue straight onto Dodge Drive. In 1.4 miles, the ranger office/visitor center will be on your left; the campground entrance is just behind this building on the left.

From Santa Fe, take I-25 North about 40 miles to Exit 323 (NM 3 South). Take NM 3 South 11.7 miles to the town of Villanueva, following the signs for the state park. Make a slight left to continue southeast on CR B29E, and in 0.3 mile continue straight (east) onto Dodge Drive. In 1.4 miles, the ranger office/visitor center will be on your left; the campground entrance is just behind this building on the left.

GPS COORDINATES: N35° 15.901' W105° 20.063'

SOUTHEASTERN NEW MEXICO

Yucca is one of the few plants you'll see growing in White Sands National Park *(see page 133)*.

28

⚠ Aguirre Spring Recreation Area Campground

Beauty ★★★★★ Privacy ★★★★ Spaciousness ★★★★★ Quiet ★★★ Security ★★★★ Cleanliness ★★★★

Rising above the Chihuahuan desert, the rocky spires of the Organ Mountains form a stunning backdrop to the campground at Aguirre Spring Recreation Area.

The creviced, craggy peaks resembled an organ's pipes, according to the European explorers who named the Organ Mountains in 1682. According to the 2014 Presidential Proclamation that established this wilderness as a National Monument, the peaks "conceal numerous ancient dwellings, including La Cueva, and other caves where smoke-blackened ceilings evidence long-extinguished campfires." Rising above the Chihuahuan desert, these rocky spires of the Organ Mountains form a stunning backdrop to the campground at Aguirre Spring Recreation Area. This beautiful campground has several great day trips and hikes nearby.

Summer would be a very hot time to camp here—with highs near 100°F and lows in the 60s—but each site has a shaded picnic table, and most have some combination of alligator juniper and Emory oak for additional shade. Mountain mahogany, sotol, and boulders add privacy to most of the sites, but some (13–20) are more open if you're wanting to keep an eye on the kids. Several sites are large enough for more than one tent, and the ground is sandy and comfortable.

The campground has the bizarre sound phenomenon where it gets so quiet you can hear a conversation several campsites away and make out nearly every word. The sun sets early behind the sawtooth Needles of the Organ Mountains, and it cools off right away. You can still enjoy the sunset by watching the vibrant stripes appear on the eastern plains of the

Level sites in the foothills see the sun set early behind the Organ Mountains.

KEY INFORMATION

LOCATION: Aguirre Spring Road

CONTACT: Bureau of Land Management, Las Cruces District Office; 575-525-4300, blm.gov/visit/aguirre-spring-campground

OPEN: Year-round

SITES: 55 single sites plus 2 group sites

EACH SITE HAS: Picnic table with shelter, fire ring; most have pedestal grills as well

WHEELCHAIR ACCESS: ADA restrooms, group picnic areas; site 45 has an accessible picnic table

ASSIGNMENT: First-come, first-served; group sites reservable

REGISTRATION: Self-register on-site or call 575-525-4300 for group sites

AMENITIES: Vault toilets, no water

PARKING: By sites; some have a 50' walk to site

FEE: $7/night ($3.50 with Interagency Pass)

ELEVATION: 5,685'

RESTRICTIONS

PETS: Permitted on leash

QUIET HOURS: 10 p.m.–6 a.m.

FIRES: In fire rings only

ALCOHOL: Permitted at sites

OTHER: No fireworks; no cutting or gathering wood. Drones prohibited near the fence line. The gate is locked at night, and only campers are permitted in the campground after 10 p.m. The gate remains open daily April–September, 7 a.m.–8 p.m.; October–March, 8 a.m.–6 p.m.

missile ranges. In the morning, the sun rises behind a hill, lighting the camp late, which is nice for late sleepers.

The first, main loop had the most campers in it when I visited, but with 55 campsites, it still felt like I had the campground to myself. Most sites don't have large enough or level enough space for RVs, and until recently the narrow, winding entrance road had a rough reputation, so there was only one RV here when I camped—and they were parked in the day-use area for the Pine Tree Trail between the two loops. The east loop has several nice sites, many of which are terraced with the picnic table above the campsite. Each loop has multiple vault toilets.

On pleasant spring and fall weekends, you may expect more traffic as Las Cruces residents picnic at sites in the main loop (the day-use fee is $5), but they'll clear out by nightfall. The spring has the added bonus of blooming cacti, but strong winds might whip your tent all day.

Aguirre Spring's camp host stays just outside the gate. Each night, the host locks the gate, primarily to keep people from having car accidents on the dark road at night. From April until September, the gate remains open from 7 a.m. to 8 p.m.; from October until March, 8 a.m. to 6 p.m.

The Organ Mountains Colorado chipmunk will likely beg you for snacks during your stay; this little chipmunk is only found in these mountains. You might also see snakes—several signs warn of rattlesnakes on the trails. Best to keep your tent zipped shut, lest any of these visitors find their way in.

The two group sites cost $50 a day to reserve. They have several picnic tables and even a grilling area complete with a prep table at group site 2. Both are accessible as far as getting to the picnic tables; there is also accessible parking and a vault toilet by the sites.

Two trails start in the gated area of the campground. The Pine Tree Trail, a 4-mile loop, starts across from site 32. The trail climbs 1,000 feet and has magnificent views when you're stopping to catch your breath. Baylor Pass Trail picks up closer to the entrance; this 5.4-mile, one-way trail will take you to Baylor Canyon. You may opt to hike to the halfway point and back. A sign in the campground warns that several people have died hiking or climbing in the mountains, and not to venture off of the trail. There's no water at the campground, so make sure you bring plenty.

The nearby Rough and Ready Hills is a popular climbing spot, with more than 40 routes for trad, sport, and toprope climbs. This area is shady in the afternoon and protected from western winds, making the volcanic tuff good for warm-weather climbing. Just don't leave water out for your dog—it will attract bees.

There's much to explore in the surrounding area, including fossils of ground sloths, rock art painted in unique styles not seen elsewhere, more than 200 ancient archaeology sites, the Butterfield Stagecoach Trail, historic sites from the Apache wars (including "Geronimo's Cave") and Billy the Kid's hideout, the Gadsden Purchase International Boundary, and the volcanic fields where astronauts trained for lunar expeditions in the 1960s. In a quiet canyon near Dripping Springs, you can find the ruins of a resort once visited by Pancho Villa, as well as the lawman Pat Garrett, who famously killed Billy the Kid. You can find out more about the area at the Dripping Springs Visitor Center, 10 miles east of I-25 off Exit 1. It's open all year—excluding winter holidays—from 8 a.m. to 5 p.m.

The nearest services are in Las Cruces, 17 miles west.

Aguirre Spring Recreation Area Campground

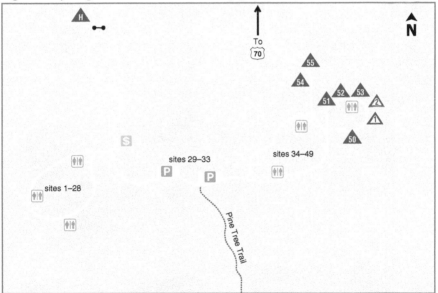

GETTING THERE

From Las Cruces, drive 17 miles east on US 70, then turn right (south) onto Aguirre Spring Road. Follow this paved road 5.5 miles to the campground, on your left.

GPS COORDINATES: N32° 22.227' W106° 33.654'

29

⛺ Caballo Lake State Park Campground

Beauty ★★★★ Privacy ★★★ Spaciousness ★★★ Quiet ★★★ Security ★★★★★ Cleanliness ★★★★★

On the opposite shore, sunrise silhouettes the Caballo Mountains and their reflection in the water.

South of Elephant Butte Lake, Caballo Lake State Park offers opportunities for canoeing, kayaking, sailing, swimming, and water skiing, as well as beach camping and boat-in camping. However, Caballo Lake is quieter and less crowded than Elephant Butte. On the opposite shore, sunrise silhouettes the Caballo Mountains and their reflection in the water; at sunset they're lit in warm colors. The name of the lake and campground come from the Sierra del los Caballos—the "jagged-ridged mountain of the horses"—which in turn were named for the herds of wild horses descended from those the Spanish brought in the 1540s. (Equestrian camping and trails remain a feature of the campground.)

The Caballo Dam, constructed from 1936 to 1938 by the U.S. Bureau of Reclamation, stretches 4,590 feet across the river and has the capacity to dam some 344,000 acre-feet of water. The dam was built to control floods and to compensate for any lost water storage capacity from Elephant Butte; water below the dam irrigates crops in southern New Mexico and fulfills the 1906 treaty obligations with the former Republic of Texas. When it's full, Caballo Lake is the third largest in the state. When I visited, the lake was at a fraction of this capacity but still filled the lakebed and was deep enough for water sports. When the water is high enough—usually during seasonal dam releases—you can put in a kayak below Elephant Butte Dam and run the 10 miles down to Caballo Lake. The park has two concrete boat ramps and three decks but no marina or rental facilities.

Bring binoculars to enjoy the great bird-watching opportunities at Caballo Lake.

KEY INFORMATION

LOCATION: Just off NM 187, Caballo, NM 87931

CONTACT: Caballo Lake State Park, 575-743-3942, emnrd.state.nm.us /SPD/caballolakestatepark.html

OPEN: Year-round

SITES: 170

EACH SITE HAS: Picnic, fire ring; electric, water, sewer hookup sites available; primitive sites have stone fire rings

WHEELCHAIR ACCESS: Sites 11, 41, 46

ASSIGNMENT: First-come, first-served and by reservation (63 sites; 877-664-7787, newmexicostateparks.reserveamerica.com)

REGISTRATION: Self-register on-site or online

AMENITIES: Showers, vault toilets, water, electricity, playground, basketball court, boat ramps

PARKING: At site

FEE: $18/night for sites with electric, water, and sewer hookups; $14/night electric and water; $10/night developed but nonelectric; $8/night primitive

ELEVATION: 4,241'

RESTRICTIONS

PETS: Permitted on leash.

QUIET HOURS: 10 p.m.-8 a.m.

FIRES: In designated areas only

ALCOHOL: At sites only; prohibited while boating

OTHER: The showers at the Riverside comfort station close seasonally, mid-October–April.

With 170 sites spread across six areas, campers have plenty to choose from. The four developed campgrounds are Appaloosa, Palomino, and Stallion, by the lake, and Riverside, by the Rio Grande. The state park offers 115 sites with water and electricity, as well as a group RV rally site. Most of these developed sites have shade pavilions set over the picnic tables and fire rings. A short lollipop hiking trail starts at Palomino Campground.

If beach camping is more your style, head to Upper Flats. This area is for primitive camping; you won't find picnic tables or pedestal grills at any of the sites. A maze of gravel roads will take you to several empty lots where you can camp. Some fire rings from gathered stones give some idea of where to pitch a tent among the salt cedar. The only toilet is near the horse corral, which is a long walk from many of the camping areas. Watch out for patches of nettles when pitching your tent along the tranquil shores—these can be a real pain for dog owners. Drive slowly on the roads here, as part of the road is shared with horses.

Percha Flats offers beach camping similar to Upper Flats. Head down the washboard road before the dam, and the road will fork at the toilet and water spigot. If you head to the right, you can camp right on the shore. Beware that some low-lying areas may flood; consult a ranger regarding current conditions.

In Riverside Campground, near the RV rally area, there's a beautiful row of tent-camping spots along the river. Each of these is mere feet from the bank, shaded by cottonwood trees, with plenty of grassy space to pitch your tent. The sites all have picnic tables and fire rings; they share two toilets. While the main loop of Riverside Campground can be bustling with RVs, the tent area is quieter, sitting about a mile from the main entrance.

From October to February, Caballo Lake teems with waterfowl, making it a good bird-watching site, particularly if you're in a kayak or canoe. Grebes, common mergansers, wigeons, mallards, and Canada geese paddle along the miles of shoreline. Increasing numbers of white pelicans have joined the great blue herons and sandhill cranes that visit. A sunburnt sign at the Riverside Campground suggests that bald eagles are among the raptors you might see while camping here; the best time to catch a glimpse of them is during the winter. On shore, roadrunners dash through campsites while hunting lizards in the creosote.

For a variety of services, head 16 miles north to Truth or Consequences. There you can fill up, eat out, grab a beer from the local brewery, or soak in one of the many privately owned hot springs.

Caballo Lake State Park Campground

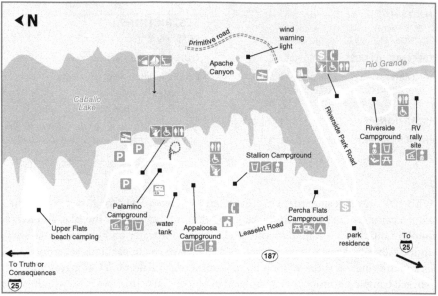

GETTING THERE

From Truth or Consequences, drive south on I-25 for 16 miles. Take Exit 59 for Caballo Lake, then turn left (north) onto NM 187, following the signs. In 1 mile, turn right to enter the park, then turn left (north) for the lakeside campgrounds or right (south) for Riverside Campground.

GPS COORDINATES: N32° 54.428' W107° 18.676'

30

Deerhead Campground

Beauty ★★★★ Privacy ★ Spaciousness ★★ Quiet ★★★ Security ★★★★★ Cleanliness ★★★★★

In a high alpine meadow, surrounded by pines and spruce, you'll find the cozy Deerhead Campground just outside of Cloudcroft.

A green getaway from the Tularosa Basin below, the Sacramento Mountains offer great hiking, stunning vistas, opportunities to view wildlife, and cooler temperatures that give reprieve from the summer heat. In a high alpine meadow, surrounded by pines and spruce, you'll find the cozy Deerhead Campground just outside of Cloudcroft.

Deerhead Campground can be a little deceptive when you first pull in. The entrance heads straight into a loop with the first eight campsites, backed against the terraced highway, which gives it a claustrophobic and exposed first impression. I nearly missed the turn to the right, between sites 1 and 2, where the rest of the sites are more evenly dispersed along the road. The first loop, nestled in a curve of the highway, is more subject to highway noise, particularly during the day; at night this road stays mostly quiet. The sites are close together in this loop, which would be nice if you wanted to occupy several with a big group of family members and friends.

Sites 3 and 14 are double sites. The camp host recommended site 2, which has plenty of shade and fits several cars. Site 16 is nice for other reasons—this site sits at the end of the loop off to the right, by itself on a slight hill overlooking a meadow filled with purple thistle.

Deerhead Campground is only a mile ouside of town, but a world away.

KEY INFORMATION

LOCATION: NM 130, Cloudcroft, NM 88317

CONTACT: Lincoln National Forest, Sacramento Ranger District, 575-682-2551, tinyurl.com/deerheadcampground; Recreation Resource Management, Inc. (concessionaire), 575-682-7570, camprrm.com/parks/deerhead-campground

OPEN: Mid-May–October 15, depending on weather

SITES: 20

EACH SITE HAS: Picnic table, fire ring

WHEELCHAIR ACCESS: Accessible toilets; at least 1 accessible site

ASSIGNMENT: First-come, first-served; no reservations

REGISTRATION: Self-register on-site

AMENITIES: Vault toilets, water fountains and spigots, trash bins

PARKING: At sites

FEE: $22/night single sites ($11 with Interagency Pass); $28/night double sites; $9/additional vehicle

ELEVATION: 8,719'

RESTRICTIONS

PETS: Permitted on leash

QUIET HOURS: 10 p.m.–6 a.m.

FIRES: In fire rings only

ALCOHOL: Permitted at sites

OTHER: 14-day stay limit; maximum 8 people/ site. Do not carve, cut, or nail into trees. Use trash bins only from 7 a.m. to 8 p.m. Generator hours: 8–10 a.m., noon–2 p.m., 5–7 p.m.

Deerhead Campground isn't just a favorite getaway for families; many animals also like to visit. Elk stroll through the campground even when it's full. Raccoons and Steller's jays look for any scraps you've left out overnight. Porcupines wander the road, so keep an eye out for them while you're driving, and keep your dog on a leash.

The concessionaire does a wonderful job of keeping the campground clean. When I visited, they had even placed solar lights with bouquets of silk flowers and hand sanitizer at each of the vault toilets. Signs were posted in English and Spanish. At the vault toilets, you'll also find water fountains and spigots with city water. The first 5 gallons are free, then the concessionaire asks for 25¢ per gallon. RVs should fill up elsewhere; they can dump at the Silver Campground station. Recycling bins are provided for aluminum only, and most of the trash cans are bear-proof. You can purchase firewood from the concessionaire for $6 a bundle.

The camp host told me that the concessionaire has placed a request with the U.S. Forest Service to make some changes to the campground—first and foremost to repair some washed out areas with rock—but these changes can be years in the making, so you may want to check the campground's status before visiting. If you arrive and it's closed, there are three other campgrounds close by, and dispersed camping is available along Forest Service Road 24B.

About 18 miles south of Cloudcroft, you can also visit the Sunspot Solar Observatory. Guided tours provide an interactive, astronomical experience; self-directed walking tours follow a 0.5-mile-loop around the facility grounds. Visitors are welcome to peer through the Dunn Solar Telescope when it is operating, which is usually weekdays from morning until midafternoon, depending on staffing. You can access the observatory from NM 6563; some digital mapping programs will tell you to turn onto unmaintained Karr Canyon Road, but that route is incorrect and may be dangerous.

If you're staying for a few days and you need to rinse off, showers are available at Silver, Saddle, and Apache Campgrounds up the road. Simply talk to the camp host at Silver Campground, and for $5 they'll turn the water on for you. For all else, you can head into

Cloudcroft, a small village with only about 700 residents. Each year, the village hosts three big festivals: the Memorial Day Weekend May Fair to kick off tourist season, the Fourth of July Jamboree, and the German-inspired Oktoberfest. At the center of the village, stop by the Burro Street Exchange, where you can eat and shop while enjoying the Old West ambience of this unique building. You can also grab a copy of the popular local newspaper, *Mountain Monthly*, to check out more local events and excursions. While driving in this area, watch out for mountain bikers and joggers on the shoulder of the highway.

Deerhead Campground

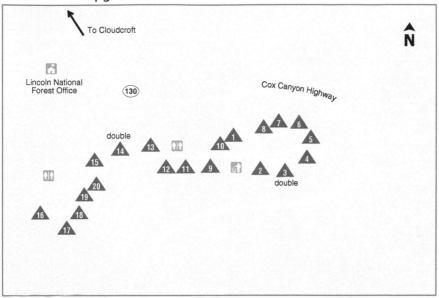

GETTING THERE

From Cloudcroft, head south on NM 130 (Cox Canyon Highway) for about 1.3 miles. The campground will be on the right.

GPS COORDINATES: N32° 56.643' W105° 44.637'

31

⛺ Fourth of July Campground

Beauty ★★★★★ Privacy ★★★ Spaciousness ★★★★ Quiet ★★★ Security ★★★★ Cleanliness ★★★★★

During autumn, the vibrant red maples at Fourth of July Campground steal the show.

In most of New Mexico, when the crisp autumn winds blow in, you can expect to see the quaking aspen turn yellow, but the forests offer few other fall colors. At Fourth of July Campground, the vibrant red maples steal the show each October, attracting crowds of photographers and day packers.

While some say the campground is so named because the vibrant leaves remind one of fireworks, others report locals once used the area to celebrate Independence Day. As one of the campgrounds close to Albuquerque, Fourth of July can be busy with campers, picnickers, and hikers, especially once the bigtooth maples change to deep red and the scrub oaks turn yellow. However, once the sun sets, the day trippers head back to town, leaving the campers with a peaceful evening.

Situated in Cibola National Forest in the Manzano Mountains, Fourth of July Campground makes for a great weekend getaway. Nicely forested, here you can enjoy the shade of ponderosa pines, spruces, junipers, oaks, and, of course, the maples. The campsites outside the loops have a touch more privacy and space than the others. Restricted to Red Canyon Campground or Manzano Mountains State Park, RVs won't be running their generators at

The trails might be packed on early autumn weekends, but Fourth of July Campground can be quieter than you'd imagine.

KEY INFORMATION

LOCATION: FS 55, Estancia, NM 87016

CONTACT: Cibola National Forest and National Grasslands, Mountainair Ranger District, 505-847-2990, tinyurl.com /fourthofjulycampground

OPEN: April–October

SITES: 23

EACH SITE HAS: Picnic table, fire ring

WHEELCHAIR ACCESS: Accessible toilets

ASSIGNMENT: First-come, first-served; no reservations

REGISTRATION: On-site

AMENITIES: Vault toilets, additional picnic area with grills; no water

PARKING: At sites

FEE: $7/night; no fee for day use

ELEVATION: 7,505'

RESTRICTIONS

PETS: Permitted on leash

QUIET HOURS: 10 p.m.–6 a.m.

FIRES: In fire rings only

ALCOHOL: At campsites only

OTHER: 14-day stay limit; no RVs

---

sunrise here. Several campers confided to me that this is their favorite tent-camping spot near Albuquerque.

Fourth of July Campground is divided into two camping loops: Gallo (16 sites) and Mosca (5 single sites, 1 double, and 1 triple). The latter loop has more spacious sites; in general, the campground is large enough that it rarely feels crowded. All sites have picnic tables, fire rings, and a parking space big enough for one vehicle.

Site 15 is particularly nice, with a little more space than its neighbors. Site 7 has a false trail that starts just behind the site and follows a creek, which can be particularly confusing for day packers—you might have some confused hikers stumble into your camp.

Plenty of Abert's squirrels make their homes in the maples and pines here, so keep an eye out for these sprightly critters. These tassel-eared squirrels change color throughout the seasons and become dark black in the fall and winter. They also might raid your campsite, so remember to secure any food or sweet-smelling toiletries before bed or a day in the forest.

There are more than 64 miles of well-developed, interlacing trails in the Manzano Mountains, and the campground boasts two short trails in addition to its small picnic area. The Crimson Maple Trail is a short interpretive trail that leads hikers through the campground. It's worth the short walk with the descriptive text in hand. This trail meets up with the Spring Loop Trail at the top of the Mosca Loop of the campground; it then joins the Fourth of July Trail and follows a stream most of the way up to the crest. The Fourth of July Trail (4.3 miles) is worth hiking in summer, too, when it's less crowded, well shaded, and dotted with wildflowers. There's no water at the campground, so pack plenty, especially if you plan on hiking to enjoy the foliage or vistas.

If you're camping here for the fall colors, you might also be able to pick fresh apples at the Manzano Mountain Retreat and Apple Ranch. *Manzano* means "apple" in Spanish, and some of the original trees the conquistadores planted still flourish here. The ranch speculates that these might the first apple trees planted in America. From mid-September through October, the Apple Ranch sells thousands of bushels of apples and gallons of cider from 37 varieties. The orchard is just south of Torreon: from NM 55 turn right onto Ten Pines Road, right at the fork, left after 0.5 mile, and finally left onto Los Pinetos.

If you happen to come up to Fourth of July Campground and find it full, or if you're looking for a smaller place to pitch your tent nearby, Tajique Campground is worth a night's stay. This small, unmarked campground is on the way to Fourth of July, about 3 miles from the turn onto Forest Service Road 55. It has a vault toilet, trash bin, and three campsites. Two campsites sit right off of the parking area; the quietest and most level site requires about a 100-foot walk upstream.

You'll find the nearest services in the town of Tajique. At Ray's you can purchase firewood and refill your water containers.

Fourth of July Campground

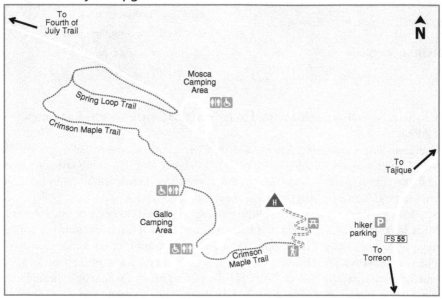

GETTING THERE

From Albuquerque, take I-40 East 14 miles to Exit 155 (Tijeras). Turn right (south) onto NM 337 South, and in 29 miles, turn right (west) at the T-intersection onto NM 55 in Tajique. Then, in 3.2 miles, turn right (west) onto FS 55 (Torreon Tajique Loop Road). The campground will be on the right after about 7.2 miles.

GPS COORDINATES: N34° 47.517' W106° 22.897'

32

⛺ Oak Grove Campground

Beauty ★★★★★ Privacy ★★★ Spaciousness ★★★ Quiet ★★★★ Security ★★★★★ Cleanliness ★★★

So-named for the stands of Gambel oak that surround most campsites, Oak Grove is peaceful, wild, and windy.

On the road to Ski Apache, before the gut-twisting hairpin turns and vertigo-inducing guard-rail vistas begin, Oak Grove Campground offers a mountainside refuge to pitch your tent. Deer and elk come right through the campground. You may even see a herd of wild horses native to the Sacramento Mountains; they graze in the nearby meadows.

The camp host recommended sites 3 and 13 because they have excellent views of the opposite hillside and you're likely to see a lot of animals near dusk and dawn. Site 3 and its adjacent sites are very open, spaced along the edge of a large meadow with only a handful of shade trees per site, but they do afford an excellent view of the hill. Site 13, a little more out of the way, is private and relaxing when the nearby, busy double site 14 isn't booked by a group. If you're willing to hike a little farther in, I'd recommend site 11, which lies on a point, surrounded by fir and hip-high yellow flowers. From between a break in the ever-green branches, I spied a small herd of deer browsing the bushes. You might also see elk and turkey.

One vault toilet was across from sites 7 and 8; another was nearer to site 19. The third vault toilet was nearer to site 25, which also had oaks large enough and perfectly spaced for a hammock. Most of the sites have been built away from the road and the small parking lots and require a short hike in—typically less than 50 feet. This slight inconvenience, though, means that the campground rates poorly on RV-camper review sites; thus, mostly tent campers fill the campground. RVs longer than 18 feet are discouraged from staying at

Some campers opt for a hammock at the aptly named Oak Grove Campground.

KEY INFORMATION

LOCATION: Just off CR 532, Alto, NM 88312

CONTACT: Lincoln National Forest, Smokey Bear Ranger District, 575-257-4095, tinyurl.com/oakgrovecampground

OPEN: May 15–October, depending on weather

SITES: 30

EACH SITE HAS: Picnic table, fire ring

WHEELCHAIR ACCESS: None

ASSIGNMENT: First-come, first-served; no reservations

REGISTRATION: Self-register on-site

AMENITIES: Vault toilets

PARKING: Near sites in shared lots

FEE: $6/night; $6/additional vehicle

ELEVATION: 8,501'

RESTRICTIONS

PETS: Permitted on leash

QUIET HOURS: 10 p.m.–6 a.m.

FIRES: In fire rings only

ALCOHOL: Permitted at sites

OTHER: 14-day stay limit; maximum 2 vehicles/site; checkout 2 p.m., 18' RV length limit

---

Oak Grove. Additionally, there's no water here. Make sure to bring at least 5 gallons—some to drink, some to cook and wash with, and some to dead-out your fire with.

While I visited Oak Grove, a U.S. Forest Service employee was investigating the mysterious continuing disappearance of the endangered Peñasco least chipmunk. One hypothesis links the continuing recreational development with the destruction of the chipmunk's habitat—specifically, subalpine meadows filled with Thurber's fescue, a grass native to these mountains. In 2019, a field biologist was trapping woodrats and mice to test for plague, suspecting that disease might play a contributing role in the chipmunk's decline. Best to obey leash laws here—if your dog chases a critter into the tall grass, he may return with an endangered animal in his maw or the plague, either of which ruin a fine camping trip.

If Oak Grove is full when you arrive, nearby South Fork Campground may be an option; otherwise, there's dispersed camping in Argentine Canyon, and you can also enjoy a light backpacking trip there. The camp host recommended against Skyline Campground (17 sites), because it's always so windy there. Monjeau Overlook is another option if you have a high clearance vehicle.

If you drive up to the ski area, there's a great, strenuous day hike (about 7 hours) to the summit of Sierra Blanca, the highest mountain in southern New Mexico (11,973'). The trailhead picks up at a parking lot at the final hairpin turn before the Ski Apache parking lot. The peak towers over the Tularosa Basin, providing stunning views of the landscape in all directions—you can see the Gila Wilderness to the west, the Sangre de Cristos to the north, and even the Guadalupe Mountains in west Texas. Because the hike summits above the tree line, it may be chilly and windy once you're taking in the views, so remember to bring a light jacket. Additionally, you may want to plan the hike to start and return before summer monsoon thunderheads gather in the late afternoon.

Should you run out of supplies, Ruidoso is close enough to easily restock and refuel. This idyllic mountain town has plenty of restaurants and tourist shops, but generally it's not too bustling—I've even seen a buck in full velvet wandering the side streets downtown, munching grass between parked cars.

Oak Grove Campground

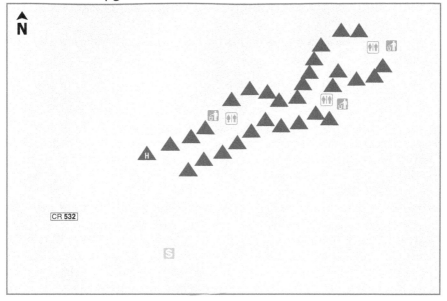

GETTING THERE

From the intersection of Main Road and NM 48 in Ruidoso, follow NM 48 North out of Ruidoso for 5.4 miles; then turn left (west) onto County Road 532 (Ski Run Road), and continue for another 5.1 miles. Just past the hairpin turn, make a right at the sign for Oak Grove, and drive 0.4 mile to the campground.

GPS COORDINATES: N33° 23.763' W105° 44.810'

A deer in velvet wanders the streets of nearby Ruidoso.

33

⛺ Percha Dam State Park Campground

Beauty ★★★ Privacy ★★ Spaciousness ★★★★ Quiet ★★★ Security ★★★★★ Cleanliness ★★★★★

The tent-camping area of Percha Dam is shaded by cottonwoods that turn a lovely yellow and come alive with cheery songs of warblers in the fall.

Percha Dam State Park lies amid farms of the fertile Mesilla Valley, along the Rio Grande. This quiet campground is 3 miles south of Caballo Lake State Park and provides more riverside camping. The tent camping area of Percha Dam is shaded by cottonwoods that turn a lovely yellow and come alive with cheery songs of warblers in the fall. All of the campsites in this park are within walking distance of the Rio Grande. In addition to birding, campers enjoy fishing, rafting, and kayaking here—or you can drive up the road to Caballo Lake for more boating activities.

Of the six Bureau of Reclamation diversion dams along the Rio Grande, Percha Dam is the only one listed on the National Register of Historic Places. This little dam, only 18.5 feet tall, was built in 1918. The diverted water flows over its top, into the Rincon Valley Canal, providing water for crops between Truth or Consequences and Las Cruces. All in all, the Rio Grande Project irrigates about 178,000 acres of crops, including the chiles and pecans southern New Mexico is known for—as well as alfalfa, corn, cotton, onion, and vineyards. As you drive into the park, you'll pass several verdant fields that also benefit from the water.

All of the reservable campsites—that is, all of the electric sites—have shade shelters over the picnic tables. Several also have stone walls around the shelters. The sites have pull-throughs to park motor homes, travel trailers, and pop-ups. A small drainage canal

Percha Dam at low-water levels

KEY INFORMATION

LOCATION: Percha Dam Canal Road, Arrey, NM 87930

CONTACT: Percha Dam State Park, 575-743-3942, emnrd.state.nm.us /SPD/perchadamstatepark.html

OPEN: Year-round

SITES: 47

EACH SITE HAS: Shade pavilion, picnic table, pedestal grill or fire ring. Some sites have short rock walls along with the shelter.

WHEELCHAIR ACCESS: Site 2 and 1 unnumbered site

ASSIGNMENT: First-come, first-served (17 sites) or by reservation (30 sites; 877-664-7787, newmexicostateparks .reserveamerica.com)

REGISTRATION: Self-register on-site or online

AMENITIES: Showers, vault toilets, water, electricity, playground

PARKING: At sites

FEE: $10/night nonelectric; $14/night electric; $18/night electric and sewer

ELEVATION: 4,447'

RESTRICTIONS

PETS: Permitted on leash

QUIET HOURS: 10 p.m.–7 a.m.

FIRES: In fire rings and grills only

ALCOHOL: Permitted at sites

OTHER: No glass containers; checkout 2 p.m.; day-use hours 6 a.m.–9 p.m; 14-day stay limit

for water runoff divides the campground from north to south, separating the electric sites from the tent sites.

On the east side of the park, along the Rio Grande, the sites are fringed with cottonwoods and willows. These sites are not numbered and are considered dispersed camping in developed sites. On the north end, four tent spots also have shelters—the rest simply have tables and fire rings, but most are shaded by the trees. These sites are nearest the dam, so you can let the sound of falling water lull you to sleep at night. Don't worry—there's also a toilet in this loop.

Like many campgrounds in New Mexico State Parks, Percha Dam has comfort stations equipped with showers, flush toilets, and sinks with running water. The upper comfort station closes seasonally, mid-October–mid-April, but the lower one remains open year-round. Water spigots are dispersed throughout the campground.

Percha Dam State Park is considered one of the top five bird-watching sites in New Mexico. In the open bosque, you may spy silky flycatchers, woodpeckers, and vireos. The campsites in the willows and cottonwoods come alive with the song of warblers during spring and fall migrations. The half-mile trail is a great meander through the riparian corridor to look for shorebirds and kingfishers. In winter, you might even see a bald eagle.

Anglers can fish for bluegill, largemouth bass, smallmouth bass, white bass, spotted bass, striped bass, and walleye. Never cross on the spillway for a better cast, and take caution picking your way across the rocks if the river is rushing—there have been drownings recently due to the swift current. Swimming is not recommended here; if you need a dip to cool off, you can head to Caballo Lake or the community swimming pool in Hatch.

In spring and summer, pack your mosquito repellent—while the birds and fish put a dent in the population, you'll be thankful for the protection. Summers can be hot, with daytime temperatures reaching 100°F and nights falling to the 70s. Monsoon rains can help cool things down in July and August.

At the visitor center, rangers plan a variety of activities each month; past events have included bird tours, stargazing programs, Easter egg hunts, as well as lectures on bats, rattlesnakes, and whiptail lizards.

If you need to restock, Percha Dam is equidistant between Hatch (20 miles south on NM 187) and Truth or Consequences (18 miles north on I-25). The Village of Hatch, the "Chile Capital of the World," hosts an annual chile festival each Labor Day weekend.

Percha Dam State Park Campground

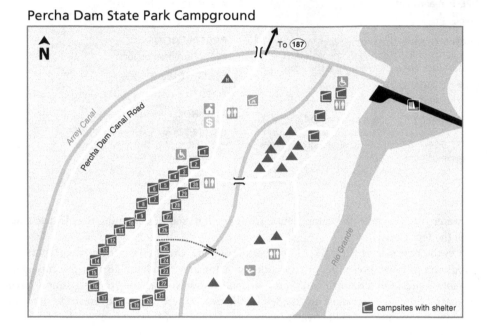

GETTING THERE

From Truth or Consequences, take I-25 South about 15 miles to Exit 59. Turn right (south) onto NM 187; then turn left (east) on East Grand Percha Road. In 0.4 mile, turn right (south) onto Percha Dam Canal Road, following the signs to the park; after 0.8 mile, the campground will be on your left.

GPS COORDINATES: N32° 52.113' W107° 18.382'

34

⛺ Pines Campground

Beauty ★★★★ Privacy ★★ Spaciousness ★★★★ Quiet ★★★ Security ★★★★★ Cleanliness ★★★★★

Pines Campground's elevation, combined with its abundance of Douglas-fir and white fir, provides relief from the summer heat, and your campsite may be visited by endangered butterflies.

Lichen mottles the bark of ponderosa pines; orange and white checkered butterflies waft on the breeze. It's hard to imagine such a beautiful campground only 1.5 miles from town, but Pines Campground is a lovely getaway for many families from El Paso, Texas, and Alamogordo, and it lies just outside of Cloudcroft. The elevation, combined with the abundance of Douglas-fir and white fir, provides relief from the summer heat, and your campsite may be visited by endangered butterflies.

Pines Campground has two "loops," but really only the Butterfly Loop qualifies as a loop—the Chipmunk Loop is more of a spur with a few sites at the end. All of the campsites are grassy and sit outside of the loop, providing a little extra space and privacy. Most sites, however, still feel open and exposed, given that there isn't much in the way of brush or small bushy trees in the campground.

Of the 24 sites, 21 are singles, 2 are doubles, and 1 is a quadruple site. Site 4, the quadruple, is a great spot for a large family or group of friends. At the end of the Butterfly Loop,

Pines Campground has sites to accommodate the whole family.

KEY INFORMATION

LOCATION: NM 244, Cloudcroft, NM 88317

CONTACT: Lincoln National Forest, Sacramento Ranger District, 575-682-2551, tinyurl.com/pinescampground; Recreation Resource Management, Inc. (concessionaire), 575-682-7570, camprrm.com/parks /pines-campground

OPEN: Mid-May–September 3

SITES: 24

EACH SITE HAS: Picnic table, fire ring

WHEELCHAIR ACCESS: Accessible toilets; at least 1 accessible site

ASSIGNMENT: First-come, first-served; no reservations

REGISTRATION: Self-register on-site

AMENITIES: Vault toilets, water fountains and spigots, trash bins

PARKING: At sites

FEE: $22/night ($11 with Interagency Pass); $28/night double sites; $42/night quadruple sites; $9/additional vehicle

ELEVATION: 8,651'

RESTRICTIONS

PETS: Permitted on leash

QUIET HOURS: 10 p.m.–6 a.m.

FIRES: In fire rings only

ALCOHOL: Permitted at sites

OTHER: 14-day stay limit; 40' RV limit; maximum 8 people/site. Do not carve, cut, or nail into trees. Use trash bins only from 7 a.m. to 8 p.m. Generator hours: 8–10 a.m., noon–2 p.m., 5–7 p.m.

---

this site spreads out into the woods with four tent pads situated under the fir boughs. It also has a shelter with two picnic tables, a large pedestal grill, and a campfire ring.

Site 23 is an interesting double site; paved with a railing, it overlooks the road and a meadow filled with bluebirds. Tent pads sit atop a slight hill just above the paved parking, picnic, and fire area.

RVs are limited to a maximum of 40 feet, but most of the parking spurs don't seem long enough to accommodate an RV of such length. The concessionaire does a wonderful job of keeping the campground clean. When I visited, they had even placed solar lights with bouquets of silk flowers and hand sanitizer at each of the vault toilets. At the vault toilets, you'll also find water fountains and spigots with city water. The first 5 gallons are free, then the concessionaire asks for 25¢ per gallon. RVs should fill elsewhere; they can dump at the Silver Campground station. Recycling bins are provided for aluminum only, and most of the trash cans are bear-proof.

In the center of the Butterfly Loop, there's a fenced meadow filled with tall grasses and a particular mix of wildflowers. According to the sign, the Sacramento Mountains checkerspot butterfly lives only in this campground and Cloudcroft; the checkerspot's range covers only 33 square miles. Even within that range, the distribution is patchy, so road maintenance, new housing subdivisions, and campground improvements could further imperil the butterfly. In this meadow you'll see New Mexico penstemon, which hosts the checkerspot's eggs, and orange sneezeweed, which produces a nectar that feeds mature butterflies.

Oshá Trail T10 connects to Pines Campground via a mountain biking trail (T568) near site 8. Named for the oshá plant, which blooms white throughout the summer along the trail, this popular trail has several vistas with benches where you can rest and appreciate the Tularosa Basin. Depending on the weather, you may be able to capture both White Sands National Monument and the Mexican Canyon Trestle Bridge in the same photograph. The main trail is a 2.1-mile lollipop and, due to the elevation, has a "moderate" rating. There are no facilities on this trail, so hike with plenty of water and pack out whatever you pack in. Please note that oshá can easily be confused with poisonous hemlocks, so it's best to leave the plant undisturbed.

If you're staying for a few days and you need to rinse off, showers are available at Silver, Saddle, and Apache Campgrounds up the road. Simply talk to the camp host at Silver Campground, and for $5 they'll turn the water on for you. The concessionaire also sells wood for $6 a bundle.

For all else, you can mosey into Cloudcroft. At the center of the village, stop by the Burro Street Exchange, where you can eat and shop while enjoying the Old West ambience of this unique building. You can also grab a copy of the popular local newspaper, *Mountain Monthly*, to check out more local events and excursions.

Pines Campground

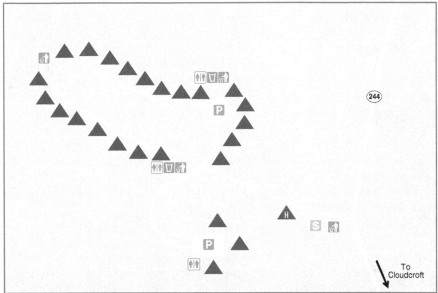

GETTING THERE

From Cloudcroft, head east on US 82 for about a mile, then turn left (northeast) onto NM 244, which will take you right to the campground, 0.5 mile ahead on the left. Lower Fir Campground is just across the road; its sign is easier to see.

GPS COORDINATES: N32° 58.002' W105° 44.128'

35

⛺ Red Canyon Campground

Beauty ★★★★★ Privacy ★★★ Spaciousness ★★★ Quiet ★★★★ Security ★★★ Cleanliness ★★★★★

The pair of campgrounds at Red Canyon makes the perfect base for exploring all that the Manzano Mountains offer.

Close to the geographic center of the state, the Manzano Mountains are at the heart of New Mexico. Part of the same fault that created the Sandia Mountains, the Manzanos are lush and full of great hikes with spectacular views. The pair of campgrounds at Red Canyon makes the perfect base for exploring all that these mountains offer either on foot or on horseback. Tall pines and thick junipers shade Red Canyon Campground all summer long. A few of the alligator junipers are so big and tall that it's fun to ponder how old they might be—these scaly junipers can live 500–800 years. You'd think that this large, lovely campground would be bustling all summer, but it's quieter than expected.

As you head up the road toward Red Canyon Campground, you'll notice the burn scar of the 2007 Ojo Peak Fire. This unseasonable fire started just before Thanksgiving and burned some 7,000 acres in just over a month. Red Canyon was spared, but the bare hills and blackened trees serve as a powerful reminder to dead out your campfire; in the Manzanos, the rugged terrain and high winds can quickly escalate human-caused embers into a stubborn wildfire. There's no water at this campground, so make sure to bring enough to drink and enough to put out your campfires.

Most sites have picnic tables and fire rings, but some also have pedestal grills. Site 11 has a table, grill, fire pit, and bear-proof food storage box; those staying at other sites will have to make do with storing their food in their car to keep critters out—notably Abert's squirrels, but bears might roam through occasionally.

A handsome flagstone firepit makes camping at Red Canyon feel like a retreat.

KEY INFORMATION

LOCATION: FS 253, 18 miles
northwest of Mountainair

CONTACT: Cibola National Forest and National
Grasslands, Mountainair Ranger District,
505-847-2990, tinyurl.com
/redcanyoncampground

OPEN: April–first snow

SITES: 38 campsites in the lower campground;
6 picnic tables and 13 equestrian sites in the
upper campground

EACH SITE HAS: Picnic table and
fire ring; some have pedestal grills,
bear boxes, or corrals

WHEELCHAIR ACCESS: Accessible restrooms

ASSIGNMENT: First-come, first-served;
no reservations

REGISTRATION: Self-register on-site

AMENITIES: Vault toilets, hiking trail access;
no water

PARKING: At sites

FEE: $7/night ($3.50 with Interagency Pass)

ELEVATION: 7,654'

RESTRICTIONS

PETS: Permitted on leash

QUIET HOURS: 10 p.m.–6 p.m.

FIRES: In fire rings and grills only

ALCOHOL: Allowed at sites

OTHER: 1 car/site; 22' RV limit;
larger vehicles must park at
Ox Canyon Trailhead, 1.5 miles south

Several sites have interesting, sunken fire pits circled by a flagstone hearth wide enough for you to pull your camping chair right up to the campfire. Most of the sites with these fire pits are inside the loop, near the restroom. Other fire pits are the more common free-standing steel rings with adjustable grates for grilling. Each restroom has two stalls and is wheelchair-accessible—however, none of the sites were explicitly designated as accessible.

Sites 8 and 9 were particularly spacious and set back from the group. In addition to their individual site amenities, this separate loop shares a big stone fire pit and a grill large enough to cook hot dogs for everyone attending your family reunion. If you do plan to invite your relatives, this would be an ideal loop to register several sites.

While the lower campground closes for winter once the first snow falls, the upper campground will remain open until snow forces the road to close. The upper campground has six picnic areas for day trippers, a group picnic spot, two toilets, and 13 sites. Each site has a corral large enough for a single horse. If you choose to camp here, you may want to pack a citronella candle and extra bug spray—where there are horses, there are horseflies.

The campgrounds connect with three hiking trails. In the lower campground, between sites 5 and 6, you'll find trailhead access for Box Spring Trail (moderate difficulty, 1.4 miles), Red Canyon Trail (rated difficult, 2.4 miles), and Spruce Spring Trail (moderate difficulty, 3.5 miles). Box Canyon leads to Ox Canyon (moderate difficulty, 3.9 miles), which then meets up with the Crest Trail and can be combined with Red Canyon for a loop. Red Canyon and Spruce Spring meet up with the Crest Trail and together can be hiked as a loop. These shady hikes afford great views, especially if you feel like scrambling up to the summit of 10,003-foot Gallo Peak. On Red Canyon Trail, two small waterfalls pour off ledges near the campground.

A sign warned that in 2019 an aggressive hawk had taken up residence on the Upper Spring Trail, about a half mile from the Crest/Spruce Trail junction. You may want to continue exercising caution on this trail, as some hawks return to the same nesting area year after year. To protect yourself from a dive-bombing hawk, you can walk with a stick

Red Canyon Lower Campground

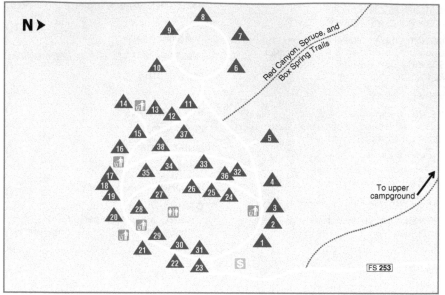

Red Canyon Upper Campground

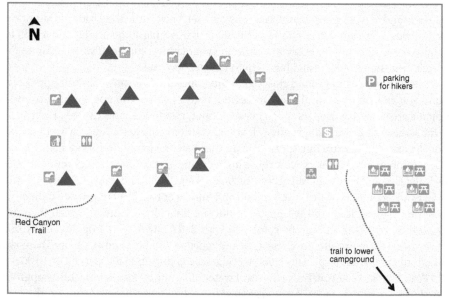

above your head—raptors will attack the tallest object rather than a person; never use the stick as a weapon.

Mountainair, about a 30-minute drive from the campground, is the closest town with a variety of services. This small town has one main street along which you can find murals and an old-fashioned ice-cream fountain. During the summer, there's likely to be a rodeo on the weekends, and in August, Mountainair hosts an annual Sunflower Festival, celebrating art and sunflowers.

GETTING THERE

From Albuquerque, take I-40 East 14 miles to Exit 155 (Tijeras). Turn right (south) onto NM 337 South, and in 29 miles, turn right (west) at the T-intersection onto NM 55 in Tajique. In 12.2 miles, bear right onto NM 131 South; in 0.1 mile, turn right again (southwest) to stay on this road. In 1.7 mile, bear right again to continue on NM 131 South, and in 0.6 mile, turn right (west) onto Forest Service Road 253. The campgrounds will be 0.7 mile straight ahead.

GPS COORDINATES: N34° 37.327' W106° 24.713'

36

⛺ Sleepy Grass Campground

Beauty ★★★★ Privacy ★★★ Spaciousness ★★★★★ Quiet ★★★ Security ★★★★★ Cleanliness ★★★★★

Sleepy Grass Campground has been regularly featured in Sunset magazine as one of the top campgrounds in the Southwest.

Just across the highway from Deerhead Campground, you'll find a much more spacious campsite at Sleepy Grass Campground. Set in a meadow stretching through mixed conifer forest, the campground has plenty of tall ponderosa pines, thick Douglas-firs draped with green moss, and the occasional Gambel oak and aspen. Sleepy Grass has been regularly featured in *Sunset* magazine as one of the top campgrounds in the Southwest. (City of Rocks, Iron Gate, Jemez Falls, Rio Chama, and Wild Rivers, also profiled in this guide, make the cut too.)

This campground is one of the most spacious I've visited in New Mexico. Twenty-one campsites are spread along a lengthy valley road; this space helps create a sense of privacy even though the open meadow and tall trees don't obscure lines of sight. Near most of the four vault toilets, you'll also find water spigots and trash cans. A larger dumpster is near site 15; the camp host asks that campers not use the bins at night due to noise. Double and triple sites are available at Sleepy Grass; you may want to check the site first to verify that it will accommodate your group. Sites 8–12 are walk-ins and sit in the open, sunny meadow. Between sites 19 and 20, an old road or trail leads farther down the valley. Mountain bikers and joggers speed through the campground and disappear down this road.

Along the slope of the southern hill, you can make out faint game trails in the trampled grass, indicating that elk and deer likely stroll into camp when it's quiet. When I camped here in the late summer, elk bugled throughout the night and coyotes yipped in the distance. In Sleepy Grass's meadows, woolly mullein grows taller throughout the summer, lit

Sleepy Grass Campground is regularly named one of the top campgrounds in the Southwest.

KEY INFORMATION

LOCATION: Apache Canyon Rd., Cloudcroft, NM 88317

CONTACT: Lincoln National Forest, Sacramento Ranger District, 575-682-2551, tinyurl.com/sleepygrass; Recreation Resource Management, Inc. (concessionaire), 575-682-7570, camprrm.com/parks/sleepy-grass-campground

OPEN: Mid-May–September 3

SITES: 21

EACH SITE HAS: Picnic table, fire ring

WHEELCHAIR ACCESS: Accessible hiking trail, toilets, at least one accessible site (site 17).

ASSIGNMENT: First-come, first-served

REGISTRATION: Self-register on-site

AMENITIES: Vault toilets, water fountains and spigots, trash bins

PARKING: At sites

FEE: $20 single sites ($10 with Interagency Pass); $28/night double sites; $36/night triple sites; $7/additional vehicle

ELEVATION: 9,013'

RESTRICTIONS

PETS: Permitted on leash

QUIET HOURS: 10 p.m.–6 a.m.

FIRES: In fire rings only

ALCOHOL: Permitted at sites

OTHER: 14-day stay limit; maximum 8 people/site. Do not carve, cut, or nail into trees. Use trash bins only from 7 a.m. to 8 p.m. Generator hours: 8–10 a.m., noon–2 p.m., 5–7 p.m.

---

with yellow blossoms. I've heard woolly mullein called "miner's candle" before, thanks to its tall stalks covered in golden florets. Western bluebirds flock to the plant, perching on the shoots and pecking out seeds.

At the entrance to the campground, you'll find La Pasada Encantada, an interactive interpretive trail for the visually impaired. Installed in the 1970s, this quarter-mile loop has 21 signs in English and Braille. In addition to counting the steps to the next sign, each one has kinesthetic and tactile information, such as "Kneel down and feel the rough texture of the decaying stump," or directions to feel the difference between the bark of a Douglas-fir and an aspen growing side by side. Some of the text, such as "no two meadows are alike," appears to paraphrase the philosopher Heraclitus.

If you're curious about the image behind the text on all of the placards, it's the Mexican Canyon Trestle, just outside of Cloudcroft. This historic landmark was once part of the Alamogordo and Sacramento Railway, which transported logs from the mountains to Alamogordo for milling and then shipped out. The railroad reached Cloudcroft in 1900, where a lodge for summer tourists was built; the town itself was also constructed with tourism in mind. Fashioned as several villages, Cloudcroft kept tourists separated from loggers and railway works. This branch of the railway was discontinued in the late 1940s. Just northwest of Cloudcroft on US 82, you can pull off the road at a great vista (near mile marker 14) to admire the cloud-climbing trestle. At the replica depot, you will also find a trailhead (Cloud-Climbing Trestle Trail No. 5001) for an easy 1.3-mile hike filled with spectacular views. You'll find a quieter and more challenging hike at the Deadman Canyon Loop Trail, just off the Sunspot Highway.

On the road to Sleepy Grass, you'll pass Aspen and Black Bear Group Campgrounds, which can be reserved by phone or online (877-444-6777, recreation.gov/camping/campgrounds/231887, recreation.gov/camping/campgrounds/231888). Both can accommodate up to 70 people, are open May 15–September 6, and cost $100 for up to 30 people and $125 for 31–70 people. The concessionaire recommends filling up water containers at Deerhead Campground (see page 105) if you plan to use these sites. Additionally, there's dispersed camping up adjacent Forest Service Road 24B.

If you're staying for a few days and you need to rinse off, showers are available at Silver, Saddle, and Apache Campgrounds up the road. Simply talk to the camp host at Silver Campground, and for $5 they'll turn the water on for you. Most other services you'll be able to find in Cloudcroft, including Wi-Fi at the Chamber of Commerce.

Sleepy Grass Campground

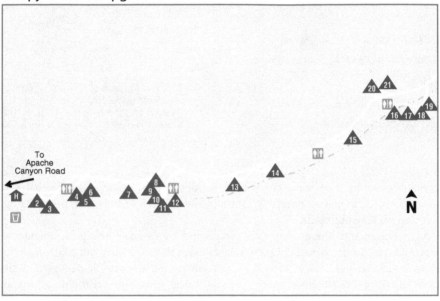

GETTING THERE

From the intersection of US 82 and NM 130 in Cloudcroft, head south on NM 130 for about 1.5 miles. Turn left (east) onto Apache Canyon Road, which will take you right to the campground, 1 mile ahead on the right.

GPS COORDINATES: N32° 56.500' W105° 44.165'

37

Sumner Lake State Park Campgrounds

Beauty ★★★★ Privacy ★★★ Spaciousness ★★★★ Quiet ★★★ Security ★★★★★ Cleanliness ★★★★★

Sumner Lake is an oasis on the plains of eastern New Mexico: deer wander the roads; bears walk the trails; birds sing from perches in mesquite and juniper.

South of Santa Rosa, in the middle of cholla-covered plains and cattle ranches, Sumner Lake State Park makes for a welcome stop on a warm day. Sumner Lake is an oasis on the plains of eastern New Mexico: deer wander the roads; bears walk the trails; birds sing from perches in mesquite and juniper. Fed by the Pecos River and dammed at the river's southern outlet, the lake provides about 6 square miles for boating, swimming, and fishing. Summer weekends fill up with adventurers from nearby Texas and the small towns of southeastern New Mexico. The water was clear and blue when I visited; you could see several feet down in the lake. Sumner Lake State Park has plenty of dispersed camping and three main camping areas: the main loop by the visitor center, the east side of the lake, and along the river.

PECOS AND MESQUITE CAMPGROUNDS (MAIN LOOP)

This nonelectric campground is a short stroll from the visitor center and comfort station. Water spigots are dispersed through the campground. These sites are spacious, and each has a shade structure and nearby cottonwood for additional shade during the toasty summers. The ground is grassy, with loose pebbles and gravel where you might pitch your tent. There is little privacy. Sites 20 and 21 have nice views of the lake. Both campgrounds have reservable sites and comfort stations with showers. On windy days, the Pecos Campground's solid shade structures make it an appealing spot to shelter your tent. A basketball hoop and playground in the Mesquite Campground are fun for kids of all ages. Nearby you'll find the

Sites along the river are grassy and shady in the summer months at Sumner Lake State Park.

KEY INFORMATION

LOCATION: 32 Lakeview Lane,
Sumner, NM 88119

CONTACT: Sumner Lake State Park,
505-355-2541, emnrd.state.nm.us
/SPD/sumnerlakestatepark.html

OPEN: East Side, April–October;
otherwise year-round

SITES: 50

EACH SITE HAS: Shade structure, picnic table,
fire ring or pedestal grill; water and electric
available in Pecos Campground

WHEELCHAIR ACCESS: Site 19;
accessible restrooms and parking

ASSIGNMENT: First-come, first-served
and by reservation (877-664-7787,
newmexicostateparks.reserveamerica.com)

REGISTRATION: Self-register on-site or online

AMENITIES: Playground, visitor center, boat
ramps, vault toilets, restrooms with water

and showers, potable water, electricity,
group campground

PARKING: At sites

FEE: $10/night nonelectric; $14/night electric;
$10/additional vehicle

ELEVATION: 4,285'

RESTRICTIONS

PETS: Permitted on leash

QUIET HOURS: 10 p.m.–7 a.m.

FIRES: In grills and fire rings only

ALCOHOL: Allowed at campsites;
no glass bottles

OTHER: 14-day stay limit; checkout at 2 p.m.
Burn only dead fallen trees; do not cut trees.
No off-road-vehicle use. Life jackets must
worn while on any flotation device, including inner tubes and floats.

Discovery Trail, a short out-and-back hike with several interpretive signs. The trail leads you from the visitor center to the overlook.

EAST SIDE CAMPGROUND

Open April 1–October 1, this campground's entrance is off NM 203 before you arrive at the main section of the park. This campground has more space for primitive camping; you can set up camp near the lakeshore. In the campground, there are a handful of electric sites and some nonelectric ones, too, along the road to the boat ramp. This campground does have potable water and a toilet. The Fox Run Trail is a fun 1.7-mile hike or bike ride that you can either use as an out-and-back or connect with the road to make a larger loop.

SHADY SIDE AND RACCOON CAMPGROUNDS (RIVERSIDE)

Just on the opposite side of the dam, you'll find the Shady Side (west side) and Raccoon (east side) campgrounds hugging the Pecos River. These two campgrounds offer a quieter camp-ing experience, away from the larger campgrounds on the lake. Large cottonwoods provide shade; thickets of salt cedar add some privacy. You can choose a grassy site for dispersed camping or pick one of the few established sites. Each site has a toilet but no water—you can fill up at one of the lake campgrounds. The state stocks the lake with walleye fingerlings; in the winter, they stock trout below the spillway into the river.

If you'd like a break from swimming, fishing, and rowing on the lake, Fort Sumner has a few notable historical attractions. Billy the Kid is buried alongside two friends under the headstone "Pals" at a small cemetery by Bosque Redondo. Due to frequent theft, the head-stone and graves are now surrounded by an iron cage—there is some irony that in death,

Billy the Kid is forever jailed. In addition to sightseeing his final resting place, you can learn more about the infamous outlaw at the Billy the Kid Museum and the Old Fort Sumner Museum, the latter of which is next to Bosque Redondo.

Bosque Redondo is now run by the New Mexico Historic Sites system and the International Coalition of Sites of Conscience, a global nonprofit that attempts to connect past struggles to current movements for human rights. A small museum explains the historical significance of the area: Fort Sumner was founded in 1862 as a U.S. Army Post built to oversee a new internment for Navajo and Mescalero Apache peoples at Bosque Redondo. Under military escort, over 8,000 Navajos were forced to march from their home 350 miles to the new fort. More than 300 people died during the "Long Walk." Five hundred Mescalero Apache were also interned. Due to alkali water, food shortages, blighted crops, and little firewood, an estimated 1,500 people died there. Close to 350 Mescalero Apache escaped to the Sacramento Mountains in 1865; the Navajo were released in 1868 when a treaty established the sovereignty of the Navajo Nation. A year later, the Army abandoned the fort and sold it to a local rancher.

Fort Sumner is a small town without many services, but you can refill on gas and buy groceries there. For a larger variety of services or to swim in the chilly waters of the Blue Hole, you'll want to head north to Santa Rosa.

Sumner Lake State Park Campgrounds

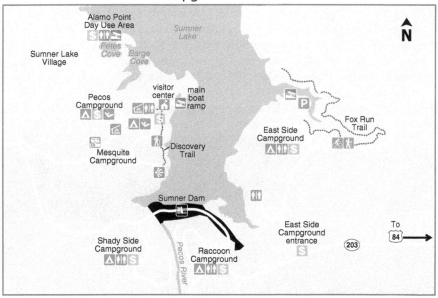

GETTING THERE

From Santa Rosa, take US 84 East toward Fort Sumner. After 34 miles, turn right (west) onto NM 203 North. Follow the signs for the park; the visitor center and main campgrounds will be across the dam, about 7.5 miles from the previous turnoff.

GPS COORDINATES: N34° 36.731' W104° 24.058'

38

⛺ Valley of Fires Recreation Area Campground

Beauty ★★★★★ Privacy ★★★ Spaciousness ★★★★★ Quiet ★★★★★ Security ★★★★ Cleanliness ★★★★

Lava spills along the edge of the campground; the field of black boulders picks up mere feet from your tent pad.

Driving down NM 380, you'll notice that the desert is interrupted by a sudden field of black basalt. Valley of Fires is one of the youngest lava flows in the continental US. Between 2,000 and 5,000 years ago, vents opened along the Tularosa Basin and lava spewed forth in overlapping flows. Geologists suspect that a majority of the basalt you see came from a small cinder cone volcano named Little Black Peak. The flow is 44 miles long and only a couple of miles wide, covering a total of 127 square miles. Wrinkled, ropy basalt called pahoehoe (pronounced "pa-hoy-hoy") suggests that several acres formed from lava with a taffylike consistency. Elsewhere, caves or tubes show that fluid lava poured forth from beneath a cooling surface.

As you drive in, you'll pass the RV sites on your way to the tent loop, where sites 20–25 and the group site are. Lava spills along the edge of the campground; the field of black boulders picks up mere feet from your tent pad. The lava arrested just shy of the campground because it's set on a hogback of Dakota sandstone with enough of an incline to make the lava pool at its base. The tent sites are very spacious, and you can easily fit an additional tent at one campsite. Site 25 may the smallest of these, but it's the most private. Built into the edge of the flow, this campsite even has a fire pit constructed in a shelf of lava, so you can watch your flames dance and cast shadows against the rock wall.

It would be tough to find a pot of gold in the field of pahoehoe at the Valley of Fires—you're better off sticking to the boardwalk to enjoy any rainbows.

KEY INFORMATION

LOCATION: 6158 US 380,
Carrizozo, NM 88301

CONTACT: Bureau of Land Management,
575-648-2241, blm.gov/visit/valley-of-fires

OPEN: Year-round

SITES: 25 campsites,
6 of which are tent-specific

EACH SITE HAS: Shade structure, picnic table,
fire ring, tent pad

WHEELCHAIR ACCESS: 2 accessible sites

ASSIGNMENT: First-come, first-served;
no reservations

REGISTRATION: Self-register on-site

AMENITIES: Fully accessible restrooms with
flush toilets, sinks, and showers in the RV

loop; vault toilets and potable water spigots
throughout park; some RV sites have water
and electric hookups; group site

PARKING: At sites

FEE: $7/night for tent camping ($3.50 with
Interagency Pass); $25/night for group site

ELEVATION: 5,710'

RESTRICTIONS

PETS: Permitted on leash

QUIET HOURS: 10 p.m.–7 a.m.

FIRES: In fire rings only

ALCOHOL: Permitted at sites

OTHER: No hunting or
off-highway-vehicle riding

Each site has a picnic table under a shade structure, a campfire ring, and one level tent pad. Across from sites 23 and 24 are the vault toilet and a water spigot. A fence runs along the sites to keep campers parking in the provided space instead of in the site.

On the opposite side of the loop, the group site has accessible parking, its own vault toilet and water spigot, six covered picnic tables, four grills, a large fire ring, and several gravel tent pads. Behind it, the sun peeks over the Sacramento Mountains as it rises.

In the campground, a few struggling cottonwoods and sycamores are watered on a drip line. Creosote, mesquite, sotol, banana yucca, bae grass, prickly pear, walking stick cholla, and hedgehog cactus sprout from cracks in the pahoehoe. Many of the small animals living here have developed blacker-than-normal skins or fur coats, while just 70 miles south, the same species have become white to camouflage themselves at White Sands National Monument. Bobcat paw prints have been seen in the fine sand near the water spigot of the tent loop, so keep your dogs close. They likely eat the cottontail rabbits and quail that dash among the broken lava. Coyotes sing all night. In the early fall, you may see tarantulas migrating.

The most annoying resident of the recreation area would be the lava gnats, as the camp host called them. Thick clouds swarm you as soon as the breeze dies down; they head for the moisture in your eyes and nose; buzz in your ears; and, if you aren't careful, may fly down your throat! The camp host advised that they are common in the late summer, which explained why I had the tent-camping loop to myself while the RV side was still bustling.

A hiking trail starts from the tent loop; you can pick it up at a break in the fence between the group site and site 25. Be aware that it quickly becomes a cell-signal dead area and the trail is unmarked; tell someone before you head out and take plenty of water. A gentler, accessible trail starts just across from the visitor center. On this 1-mile loop, 14 interpretive signs guide your viewing and provide background information on this stunning geology and ecosystem.

The visitor center has books on geology and local flora and fauna, postcards, a mail drop, and information about New Mexico's public lands. If you forgot one, you can buy a hat here, too, but for anything else, you'll probably have to head into Carrizozo. This town, named for a reed (the carrizo; the extra -zo was added to indicate how bountiful the reed was at the end of the 19th century) is about 4 miles south, at the intersection of 380 and 54.

Nearby attractions include the ghost town of White Oaks, where Billy the Kid's gun-slinging escalated; Three Rivers Petroglyph National Site, which has one of the largest collections of petroglyphs in the country; and the home and final resting place of Smokey Bear, in Capitan, New Mexico.

Valley of Fires Recreation Area Campground

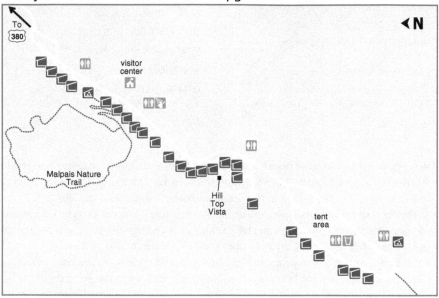

GETTING THERE

From Socorro, drive south on I-25 about 9 miles, and take Exit 139 for US 380 East toward San Antonio and Carrizozo. Continue east for 61.2 miles, and the recreation area will be on your right.

GPS COORDINATES: N33° 41.088' W105° 55.198'

39

White Sands National Park Campground

Beauty ★★★★★ Privacy ★★★★★ Spaciousness ★★★★★ Quiet ★★★★★ Security ★★★★★
Cleanliness ★★★★

Play in the sand, sled down dunes on waxed sleds, grab your camera to document the light and shadow on the dunes, or simply enjoy the solitude of the bright white field—White Sands offers something for everyone.

There's no other place like White Sands National Park on Earth—one of our newest national parks is a unique ecosystem in the world's largest dunefield. The park is 275 square miles of rolling dunes, some of which are 45 feet high and might travel close to 38 feet per year. The glistening, silky white sand is actually a mineral deposit called gypsum; it doesn't absorb heat like sand does, so it's always cool and pleasant to dig your feet into the soft belly of a dune.

Picturesque and awe-inspiring, White Sands presents an unparalleled tent camping experience. Fall is the perfect time of year to camp here; spring is pleasant, too, but winds can create white-out conditions, making it easy to get lost.

Play in the sand, sled down dunes on waxed sleds (available for purchase at the gift shop, which also has a buy-back program for well-kept sleds), grab your camera to document the light and shadow on the dunes, or simply enjoy the solitude of the bright white field—White Sands offers something for everyone. Sunsets and sunrises are stunning here; full moons will take your breath away.

After thousands of generations, spanning 7,000 years, several animal species have adapted to the blanched environment and are now white. You may encounter the following camouflaged

You might want to pack a camera to photograph the unparalleled beauty of the dunes at sunset.

KEY INFORMATION

LOCATION: Dunes Drive off US 70, about 15 miles southwest of Alamogordo

CONTACT: White Sands National Park, 575-479-6124, nps.gov/whsa

OPEN: Year-round

SITES: 10

EACH SITE HAS: A site marker and a beautiful view

WHEELCHAIR ACCESS: None at campground, but the Interdune Boardwalk is an accessible interpretive trail

ASSIGNMENT: First-come, first-served; no reservations

REGISTRATION: At visitor center; permit required

AMENITIES: None

PARKING: In lot, 1 mile from sites

FEE: Entrance fee ($25/vehicle) plus $3/person; 50% discount with an Interagency Pass

ELEVATION: 4,235'

RESTRICTIONS

PETS: Permitted on leash no longer than 6 feet

QUIET HOURS: Not posted

FIRES: Not permitted (fire can damage gypsum sand crystals and burn the organic soil)

ALCOHOL: No stated restrictions

OTHER: You may only camp 1 night at a time; vacate by 1 p.m.; maximum 6 people/site. If there is more than 1 vehicle in your group, all vehicles must be present to get a permit.

---

critters: white Apache pocket mouse, bleached earless lizard, sand-treader camel cricket, sand wolf spider, or white moths. Occasional plants pop out of a dune: tall soaptree yucca, pedestals of skunkbush sumac, and purple sand verbena all hang to life in this arid ecosystem.

Backcountry Camping Trail is a 2-mile loop. There's no defined trail (the sands are always shifting), so you follow a series of orange stakes with spades painted on them. The dunes along this trail are large, and there are fewer plants, so finding the trail markers is easy. Packing your gear up the steep side of a dune, with your feet digging into the loose sand with each step, can challenge some campers.

Each site is numbered and has a post to designate where to set up your tent. Site 5 is the farthest out, so it's just you and the dunes and the yawning sky. A sleeping pad is a must: the gypsum becomes as hard as concrete and freezing cold at night.

Pack in plenty of water; you can fill up at the visitor center. Rangers recommend that if it's already over 85°F, you shouldn't start the hike out to the campsites because it may be too hot and dangerous. Before you hike out, use the restroom at the parking lot—there's no toilet in the dunes. To avoid hiking back and forth from the toilet, you can purchase a human-waste disposal bag to pack it out, or make sure you bury waste at least 100 feet from the trail/campsite and 3–6 inches deep.

During the white-hot truce of noon in the summer, temperatures peaking above 100°F are common—as are sunburns and the symptoms of hyperthermia. The white sand reflects sunlight, so the park rangers recommend long sleeves, pants, wide-brimmed hats, and plenty of sunscreen. Heat-related illness has been fatal here in the past. See page 11 for more information.

In addition to the heat and exposure in White Sands, a host of other potential hazards can surprise you if you aren't prepared. Before you head out to the monument, you'll want to check the missile-closure schedule: Dunes Drive may be closed for hours at a time during missile tests. Camping will be prohibited the night before these closures. You may also find unexploded ordnance left over from a test or debris from a missile half-buried in the sand.

These may still be active, so if you see any strange objects, tell a ranger. Also, GPS may be unreliable in the monument; keep a compass on hand, pick up a map at the visitor center, and make landmarks from notches in the mountains to stay oriented.

Several short hikes show off different areas of the park. The 0.4-mile Interdune Boardwalk has 10 interpretive signs to teach visitors about the ecology and geology of "the world's greatest sandbox." The 0.5-mile Playa Trail has additional interpretive exhibits in an area of the park that may be brown, white, or growing crystals. The mile-long Dune Life Nature Trail introduces families to the park's animals. The most strenuous of the hikes, the Alkali Flat Trail, is a 5-mile walk up and down dunes skirting the remnant of ancient Lake Otero—it takes about 3 hours to hike, and this trail isn't for the faint of heart.

On the monument website, you can schedule a tour of Lake Lucero; join a ranger for a full-moon hike; or sign up for a sunrise arts experience, where you can photograph, draw, or paint the dunes in the first rays of dawn.

With only 10 sites, the campground fills up fast, so you'll want to get to the visitor center as soon as it opens at 7 a.m. I recommend camping at Oliver Lee Memorial State Park (26 miles) outside of Alamogordo the night before, so you'll be close enough to get there first thing in the morning; you could also camp at Aguirre Spring, 40 miles east of Las Cruces (see page 99). Alamogordo and Las Cruces are also your closest options for services.

White Sands National Park Campground

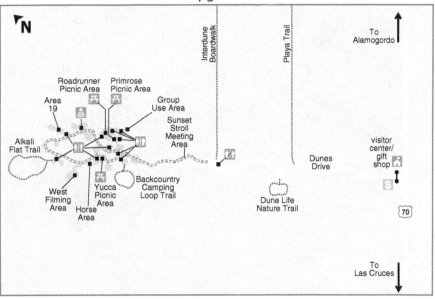

GETTING THERE

From the intersection of US 54 and US 70 in Alamogordo, drive southwest on US 70. After 14 miles, turn right (west) onto Dunes Drive/Loop Drive, following the signs for White Sands. The camping area is about 6.5 miles ahead, on your left.

GPS COORDINATES: N32° 48.422' W106° 16.498'

SOUTHWESTERN
NEW MEXICO

The view from Water Canyon Campground lets you watch your friends arrive
(see page 167).

40

⛺ Apache Creek Campground

Beauty ★★★★★ Privacy ★★★ Spaciousness ★★★★★ Quiet ★★★ Security ★ Cleanliness ★★★

You may spot the threatened Chiricahua leopard frog here along the banks of the creek or leaping through the cattails at one of ponds.

Apache Creek Campground is a lovely, quiet campground surrounded by willows and ponderosa pines. The area has a rich history of ancient Puebloan residence; near here you'll find the Apache Creek Ruin, a collection of pit houses erected between 1150 and 1300 C.E., as well as many petroglyphs. More-recent history includes the Apache resistance fighters Mangas Coloradas, Victorio, Geronimo, Chato, and Cochise; down the road is the site of the Alma Massacre of 1880.

Now you'll find the sleepy town of Apache Creek, population 67. A one-lane bridge crosses the lazy creek, which pools into small, serene ponds. Ponderosa pines stand silent, barely moving in the breeze. Willows grow bright yellow in the fall, contrasting with black chunks of basalt. Along the banks of the creek, or leaping through the cattails at one of the ponds, you may even spot the threatened Chiricahua leopard frog. Listen for the sound of snoring and you may see this large, stocky, spotted frog—they can even call while underwater!

Purple asters and petite yellow flowers cover the campground. For several years, this campground was completely undeveloped, dispersed camping, and the practice was simply to pull up to your favorite ponderosa pine and pitch your tent. Now each of the 10 sites has the standard picnic table and campfire ring with a grill; a few sites also have shade structures or benches carved from felled ponderosa pines. Many are situated under choice pines and have ample shade. Some campers still make their own sites a little way from the

Near Apache Creek Campground, a small hill is home to several petroglyphs.

KEY INFORMATION

LOCATION: Just southwest of the junction of NM 12 and FS 94, Apache Creek, NM 87820

CONTACT: Gila National Forest, Reserve Ranger District, 575-533-6231, tinyurl.com/apachecreekcampground

OPEN: Year-round

SITES: 10

EACH SITE HAS: Picnic table, fire ring; some have shade structures and benches

WHEELCHAIR ACCESS: Accessible toilet

ASSIGNMENT: First-come, first-served; no reservations

REGISTRATION: Self-register on-site

AMENITIES: Vault toilet; no trash service or water

PARKING: At sites

FEE: Free

ELEVATION: 6,448'

RESTRICTIONS

PETS: Permitted on leash

QUIET HOURS: 10 p.m.–6 a.m.

FIRES: In fire rings only

ALCOHOL: Allowed at sites

OTHER: 14-day stay limit; no saddle, pack, or draft animals; no fireworks

loop. If you do set up a dispersed camp, choose a spot at least 200 feet from any water. Also, remember that campfires are only permitted in the provided fire rings.

While Apache Creek Campground does have a vault toilet in the main loop, no trash service is offered, so pack out whatever you pack in. There's also no potable water available at this location, so plan to bring plenty to drink, cook, clean, and dead-out your fire with.

The whole campground is fairly level and easy to drive. Given its proximity to the highway, flat sites, and ease of access, RVers frequent this campground, especially in the fall once hunting season starts.

If you're looking for a nice stroll with the opportunity to view archaeological evidence from hundreds of years ago, you can head to the Apache Creek Interpretive Trail 16. From the campground, you can walk a quarter of a mile down Forest Service Road 94; the trailhead will be on your left. When I visited, the trail didn't look like it got much traffic, so during more lush times of year, it may be more difficult to spot. The trail is a loop a little less than a mile long, with almost 200 feet of elevation change. At the apex of the loop, you'll see several petroglyphs pecked into the basalt wall. Do not touch the petroglyphs—even tiny amounts of oil from your hands can erode the images.

Another petroglyph trail, Walk in the Past Trail 616, offers a moderate, 3-mile round-trip hike that passes by an old Tularosa Ranger Cabin and a number of Mogollon period glyphs on the southwest-facing volcanic escarpment along the Tularosa River. To get there, drive 2 miles south on NM 12, and take a left on the road with the blue cattle guard; you should see a sign with a hiker symbol.

Another popular nearby trail is Frisco Divide Trail 762. This difficult, 7-mile-long trail follows a slot canyon that leads to Warm Springs Trail, where you can soak in one of two concrete tubs built on the springs. The trail crisscrosses the chilly San Francisco River, which adds considerable time to the hike. The tubs are not managed; soak at your best judgment. Beware of flash floods, especially during monsoon season. For a more relaxing adventure, just 32 miles north on NM 32, you can fish at Quemado Lake.

Back at the junction with NM 12, a little store offers taxidermy, among other services. Many campers report pleasant conversations with the owner about the history of the area.

If you can't find what you need there, you can head to Reserve, about 13 miles southwest. There you'll find several restaurants, a gas station, grocery store, and a medical clinic.

Apache Creek Campground

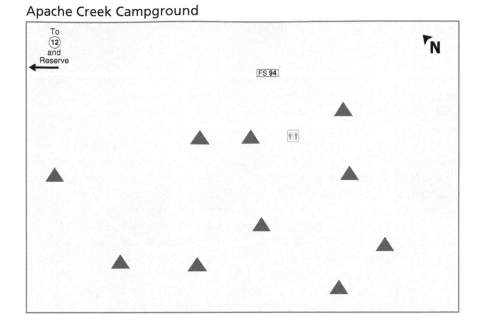

GETTING THERE

From the intersection of NM 435 and NM 12 in Reserve, drive northeast on NM 12. In about 12 miles, just past mile marker 19, turn right (south) onto FS 94. In about 200 feet, turn left to reach the campground entrance.

GPS COORDINATES: N33° 49.734' W108° 37.638'

41

⛺ City of Rocks State Park Campground

Beauty ★★★★★ Privacy ★★★★ Spaciousness ★★★★ Quiet ★★★★★ Security ★★★★★ Cleanliness ★★★★★

In the middle of the Mimbres River Valley, a strange formation of boulders juts up, forming the City of Rocks.

City of Rocks State Park is one of my favorite early-fall/late-winter camping spots in New Mexico. The "city" was formed 34.9 million years ago, when the Kneeling Nun volcano erupted, spewing hot ash into the air. This eruption is estimated to have been 1,000 times larger than that of Mount St. Helens, and to have lasted for several years. The hot ash settled in thick layers, forming solid tuff; as it cooled, it shrank, creating vertical cracks. The wind and rain have been sculpting pinnacles and boulders ever since. Some of the rock columns reach 40 feet high; they range from light brown to pink in color. Narrow footpaths cut around them and could be explored all day. Compared with the low Mimbres River Valley that surrounds it, the geologic wonder is an abrupt, surprising feature of the landscape. Boulder formations like these exist in only six sites across the world.

Rangers host frequent star parties at the Gene and Elisabeth Simon Observatory, near the Orion group area (in addition to being numbered, each site has an intergalactic name). The observatory consists of a 14-inch Meade LX-200 telescope that sits permanently in a 12-by-16-foot building with a roll-off roof. Star parties usually align with new moons, when you can see more stars. As you might guess, you don't need access to the telescope, or the perfect moon, to enjoy clear nights picking out constellations and planets from the blanket of stars.

City of Rocks is also teeming with wildlife. In addition to the usual suspects—black-eared jackrabbits, cottontails, and prairie dogs—I've also seen plenty of tarantulas, owls,

Prickly pear in the botanical garden resemble the shapes of the volcanic formations that make City of Rocks such an interesting camping spot.

KEY INFORMATION

LOCATION: 327 NM 61, Faywood, NM 88034

CONTACT: City of Rocks State Park, 575-536-2800, emnrd.state.nm.us /SPD/cityofrocksstatepark.html

OPEN: Year-round

SITES: 45 tent sites

EACH SITE HAS: Flat tent area, fire ring, picnic table. Many sites also have trash cans, as well as boulders and Emory oaks that provide shade.

WHEELCHAIR ACCESS: Accessible restrooms

ASSIGNMENT: First-come, first-served and by reservation (8 sites; 877-664-7787, newmexicostateparks.reserveamerica.com)

REGISTRATION: Register on-site or online

AMENITIES: Water, pit toilets, restrooms with running water and showers by the visitor center

PARKING: Near sites; maximum 2–5 vehicles/ parking spot, depending on-site

FEE: $8/night

ELEVATION: 5,231'

RESTRICTIONS

PETS: Permitted on leash except inside visitor center

QUIET HOURS: 10 p.m.–7 a.m.

FIRES: In fire rings only

ALCOHOL: Permitted

OTHER: Gate is closed each night from 9 p.m. to 7 a.m.; do not climb boulders

---

and bats. In the spring of 2016, a pair of kit foxes raised a litter of five pups next to the RV electrical hookup sites. Badgers have been spotted near the Orion group area. As you climb around the boulders, watch out for rattlesnakes.

Between sites 34–38, you'll find evidence of the park's ancient past. Several of the rocks have been used as grinding stones. Some also have small, conical wells to collect rainwater. The Mimbres people hunted and camped here as late as 800 years ago. Pottery sherds, arrowheads, and stone tools have also been found in the area.

Most of the campsites have some combination of boulders and trees protecting the area that has been leveled for tents. The Emory oaks retain their leaves throughout winter, providing shade year-round. Several sites have their own trash cans in addition to fire rings and picnic tables. Due to the nature of the "city," water runoff is great during storms—it flows through the channels between boulders. Sites 15–19 form the Pegasus Campground and can be reserved online. Just behind site 32, in a narrow slot, there's a hidden Kokopelli pictograph in a small cavity caused by a gas bubble in the tuff. It's at about eye-level and usually protected from the elements by a flat rock. I surprised both myself and a Texas horned lizard the last time I found the painting.

As with many of the state parks, you can also take a shower here—there's a comfort station by the visitor center, which also has bathrooms with running water.

Near site 45, the Hydra Trail (3.25 miles) starts with a small botanical garden, then loops around the campground. A spur (0.5 mile) leads you out to the observation point, overlooking the "city" and the Chihuahuan desert prairie. Another spur (1.56 miles) takes you to the top of Table Mountain. The elevation there is 5,726 feet and also provides another great view. The "Planet Walk" cuts through the boulders, meandering the narrow slots. Just outside the park, Cienega Trail makes a 2-mile loop through the desert.

The desert livens up in the spring, when the cacti start blooming in a spectrum befitting the color wheel. White jimsonweed, blue vervains, orange globemallows, and pink four o'clocks add more color to the trail. Summer temperatures can soar over 100°F; bring plenty of water with you on hikes and meanders through the boulders, and know the signs of dehydration and hyperthermia (see page 11).

Once you've finished hiking for the day, you may want to stop at the nearby Faywood Hot Springs. The hand-built resort has 14 geothermal pools you can soak in ($13 per day), some of which are clothing-optional. Several peacocks live there, so dogs must remain leashed. You can also camp here if City of Rocks has filled up. The sites are close together, but they are hidden in a thicket of trees to create privacy. I camped here one night and was delighted to find nesting mourning doves in the branches above my picnic table.

At the visitor center, you can purchase firewood, ice, and propane, as well as an assortment of toiletries, field guides, and hats. Otherwise, the closest cities with food and amenities are Deming (27 miles southeast) and Silver City (30 miles west).

City of Rocks State Park Campground

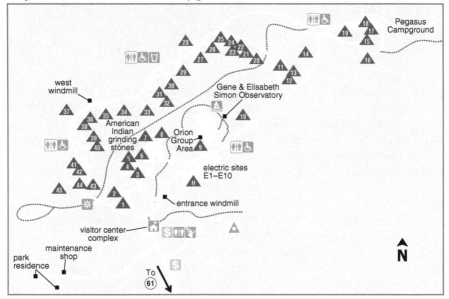

GETTING THERE

From the intersection of I-10 and US 180 in Deming, drive northwest on US 180 North. After 24 miles, turn right (northeast) onto NM 61 North. Continue for another 3.2 miles; the entrance to the park is straight ahead.

From the intersection of NM 90 and US 180 in Silver City, head east on US 180. After 27.3 miles, turn left onto NM 61 North, and proceed as above.

GPS COORDINATES: N32° 35.271' W107° 58.489'

42

Datil Well Campground

Beauty ★★★★ Privacy ★★★★ Spaciousness ★★★ Quiet ★★★★ Security ★★★★★ Cleanliness ★★★★★

Surrounded by the Plains of San Agustín, Datil Well Campground once provided water and relief for cattle herders.

If you close your eyes, you might be able to imagine the lowing of the cattle driven across the Plains of San Agustín. Beginning in 1885, when the railroad branch line at Magdalena was completed, ranchers from eastern Arizona and western New Mexico would trail their cattle and sheep past here to the railhead. In 1919, some 150,000 sheep and 21,677 cattle were driven through here, making it a peak-trailing year. Because water here tends to run west from the Continental Divide, draining to the Pacific Ocean, droughts are common in this part of western New Mexico. To make it easier to drive cattle and keep them watered, the Civilian Conservation Corps (CCC) drilled wells every 10 miles for the livestock; this campground was originally one of those watering holes. The Magdalena Trail was still in use until the 1970s.

As soon as you step out of the car, you can smell the juniper; one-seed, Utah, alligator, and Rocky Mountain varieties all seem to be present at this campground. There's also an abundance of soaptree yucca and datil, as the name of the campground implies. Many sites have pull-through parking, which gives them more seclusion, and several have shade structures. The ones that lack shade structures still have plenty of shade from mature juniper

From the overlook, you may spy pronghorn playing in San Augustine Plains below.

trees. All of the sites have picnic tables, grills, and fire rings. Any dead and downed firewood found within the campground can be collected and used for your campfire.

Three new vault toilets are easily accessible from any site, and several water spigots are dispersed around the loop. The water from these spigots comes from one of the original wells that the CCC drilled for the Magdalena Stock Driveway. At the small visitor center across from the camp host site, there is more information about the history of this area, as well as Wi-Fi.

Throughout the campground, several interpretive markers explain the difference between the varieties of yucca and juniper growing here. Starting at the gazebo between sites 6 and 8, a double-looped set of trails begins. The 3.5-mile hike leads you to three nice overlooks, two of which have small sheltered benches to provide a break from the sun and wind. From the San Agustín Overlook, you can search the plains below for pronghorn antelopes (which aren't actually antelopes but a related species) and the radio telescopes that make up the Very Large Array (VLA).

The VLA is worth a visit. Just 15 miles east of Datil, 27 radio telescopes seek the cosmos's boundaries, observe black holes, and sometimes detect unexplained phenomena around brown dwarfs. In the frequencies they pick up, they could one day uncover distant civilizations. Visitors are permitted to walk around one telescope, crane their necks looking at the massive antennae, and ponder the mysteries of our universe. A small visitor center hosts tours on the first and third Saturdays of each month.

I camped here in the spring to use the site as a base for rock climbing The Enchanted Tower, which is in the Datil Mountains in Cibola National Forest to the northwest. If you've come to climb, I would recommend using the easement to access the Thompson Canyon, where the climbs are hidden. The U.S. Forest Service access road makes for a tough ride in a passenger car. The mountains are rugged, steep, and remote—you'll see few other climbers or hikers in this wilderness.

If you have a sweet tooth, make sure to stop in nearby Pie Town to pick up a freshly baked pie from one of the many eateries along the highway. Pie Town also has roots in the livestock industry: an industrious baker named Clyde Norman, who made pocket-size apple pies for cowboys to eat while they drove cattle on to Magdalena, founded the town based on the reputation of his confections. Now only about 200 people live in Pie Town, but several bakeries line the highway and sell pies in both personal and shareable sizes. Each September, on the second Saturday of the month, the town hosts a Pie Festival, where bakers compete for the titles of Pie King and Queen.

The nearest services to the campground are in Datil, just 1 mile east. There you can load up on gas, ice, and convenience-store snacks. On weekends, the local restaurant may also have live music. For anything more substantial or more difficult to find, plan to visit Socorro.

Datil Well Campground

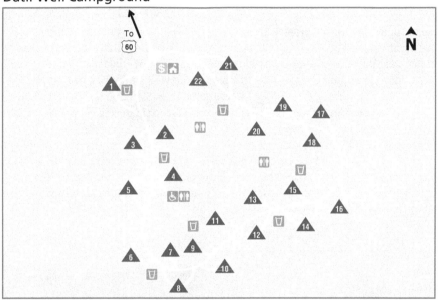

GETTING THERE

From Socorro, drive west on US 60 for about 62 miles. Continue 1 mile past the town of Datil, and the campground will be on the left.

GPS COORDINATES: N34° 09.257' W107° 51.485'

43

Dipping Vat Campground at Snow Lake

Beauty ★★★★ Privacy ★ Spaciousness ★★★★★ Quiet ★★★ Security ★ Cleanliness ★★★★

When you stay at Dipping Vat Campground, make sure to spend some time gazing at the immense spread of stars above, picking out constellations, and watching shooting stars and satellites zip across the nearly 360° view of the sky.

This hilltop campground is open, grassy, and scattered with ponderosa pines. While the few giant pines do little for privacy, the absence of much tree cover affords a majestic view of the night sky. When you stay at Dipping Vat Campground, make sure to spend some time gazing at the immense spread of stars above, picking out constellations, and watching shooting stars and satellites zip across the nearly 360° view of the sky. The nearby Cosmic Campground is one of only 10 certified International Dark Sky Sanctuaries in the world, but for less-primitive camping, Snow Lake is the next best place in the Gila National Wilderness to ponder and observe the universe.

Two connected loops atop the hill overlooking Snow Lake form the entirety of Dipping Vat Campground. Most sites have a tall ponderosa pine for shade, but the ones without are exposed and open. Sites 2 and 40 have enough young blackjack ponderosas that you can hang a hammock or even some tarps, if you're so inclined. Sites 11, 12, and 13, on the eastern loop, have spectacular views of the lake.

Clouds and stars reflect in the water at Snow Lake.

KEY INFORMATION

LOCATION: FS 1421, Reserve, NM 87830

CONTACT: Gila National Forest,
Reserve Ranger District, 575-533-6231,
tinyurl.com/dippingvat

OPEN: Year-round

SITES: 40

EACH SITE HAS: Picnic table, fire ring

WHEELCHAIR ACCESS: None

ASSIGNMENT: First-come, first-served;
no reservations

REGISTRATION: Self-register on-site

AMENITIES: Potable water, vault toilets, trash
bins, boat ramp; some sites have pedestal grills

PARKING: At sites

FEE: $5/night

ELEVATION: 7,421'

RESTRICTIONS

PETS: Permitted on leash

QUIET HOURS: 10 p.m.–6 a.m

FIRES: In fire rings only

ALCOHOL: Permitted at sites

OTHER: 14-day stay limit; no OHVs/ATVs;
no hunting. Do not clean animals or fish in
the water spigots. Trash service is seasonal
(April–November). No hookups; camping
trailers over 19' not recommended.

Site 33 has had some recent drainage work done; rainfall should now flow into the small ditch adjacent to the parking spur. This site, and 32 and 35 near it, feel bare due to the construction but should seem complete in a season or two.

Trash is only collected April–November; if you camp here December–March, plan to pack out your trash. Four spigots pump water for drinking or cooking; you may want to filter this water before consuming it.

The vault toilets are interesting adobe brick buildings, and the one on the western loop doesn't appear ADA-accessible. Down at the lake, you'll find a set of more typical vault toilets, which are accessible. The fishing pier is also accessible.

Snow Lake is stocked with trout three times each year: early spring, early summer, and late fall. Here you have the opportunity to hook one of the rarest trout species in the country: the Gila trout. Only 17 populations of this golden trout exist in the wild; thanks to significant effort to restore its numbers, this once-endangered fish is now managed as a sportfish in select locations around the state. Anglers must have a New Mexico fishing license to fish; you can pick one up in Reserve at the Adobe Cafe and Bakery or Adobe Does Cafe.

In the late summer, low water levels, combined with high heat, can cause algae blooms along the shoreline. Check the water before swimming, drinking, or letting your dog play in it—if it appears too green or has mats of algae, don't consume it or submerge it in it. You can, however, continue to eat fish pulled from the lake as long as you clean them.

On Forest Service Road 28, toward Mogollon, there are several hiking opportunities. The Gila National Wilderness is home to 56 native varieties of trees; hiking along Willow Creek Trail 154, you'll see a beautiful gallery of willows along the banks, mixed among the conifers more expected at such a high altitude. You'll find two picturesque but small campgrounds farther down the forest road. Willow Creek has only four sites, tucked among thickets of willow and spruce. You must ford the creek to access the campsites, which may be difficult after heavy rains. Ben Lilly has five sites, each gorgeous and level, spread among tall pines and firs. The gentle creek babbles along the edge of the campground, making a nice area for kids to fish and play.

While my brand-new atlas made it appear as though the road to Mogollon connected with FS 28 past Ben Lilly, the road really does dead-end at Willow Creek Ranch. You'll find the turnoff at Willow Creek Campground. Before heading that way, check that the way to Mogollon is open—it frequently closes and is impassable for low-clearance vehicles.

Although the road to Dipping Vat Campground is paved for part of the way, when I visited it was full of potholes and required constant attentiveness while driving. Plan for a 2-hour drive. Even so, driving with cautious navigation, I blew a tire and then the donut; a woman I spoke with in Reserve said the potholes have been there so long, she has them memorized. Luckily, there are several places in the tiny town of Reserve to fix a flat. Jesse's Tire Shop even helped me out on a Saturday night, restoring my faith in the kindness of strangers. Even though it's a town of fewer than 300 people, Reserve will have most of what you need if you run low on anything: there are two small grocery stores, a hardware store, a bar, and a gas station.

Dipping Vat Campground at Snow Lake

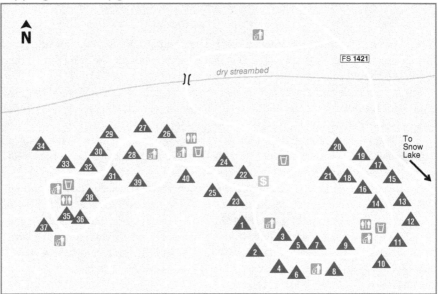

GETTING THERE

From the intersection of NM 12 and NM 435 in Reserve, head south on NM 435/Forest Service Road 141 for 34 miles; then turn right (southeast) onto NM 159. After 3.9 miles, turn left (east) onto FS 142 (Loco Mountain Road); this road will become FS 1421 and will end at the campground after about 7 miles.

GPS COORDINATES: N33° 25.380' W108° 30.062'

44

⛺ El Malpais National Conservation Area: JOE SKEEN CAMPGROUND

Beauty ★★★★ Privacy ★★★ Spaciousness ★★★ Quiet ★★★★★ Security ★★★★ Cleanliness ★★★★★

Discover the land of fire and ice when you spend the night at Joe Skeen.

Cinder cones, shield volcanoes, and lava flows dominate the landscape southeast of Grants, New Mexico. Known as El Malpais, or "the bad country," this lava field has more than 100 individual volcanoes. As you drive along the highway, you'll start to notice the land broken up by black rock, and once you turn into the park, the lava stretches as far as the eye can see. Two types of lava exist in the park: *pahoehoe* (pronounced "paw-hoey-hoey") and *'a'a* (pronounced "ah-ah"). Pahoehoe develops from slow-moving lava and has a smooth surface; often it's rippled or ropy in appearance. 'A'a rips out of the earth quickly, mixing with sediment, shearing and twisting along; it has a rough surface and can be tricky to walk on. In the geologic scale of time, some of the eruptions are quite young—the most recent being a mere 3,000–4,000 years ago.

Vegetation is beginning to cover the rough and ropy black basalt. The oldest Douglas-fir trees in the American Southwest live in the basalt lava flows on the west side of the park.

Across the road from the lava flows, Joe Skeen Campground lies on a gentle slope backed by a small cliff face on the eastern edge. Each site in this high desert campground is nestled among juniper, cholla cactus, and yellow chamisa. The campground itself might seem plain, but it's in perfect striking distance for a multiday adventure in the beautifully rugged El Malpais National Monument and Conservation Area.

La Ventana Arch is a sandstone marvel in an area better known for impressive lava fields.

KEY INFORMATION

LOCATION: NM 117, Grants, NM 87020

CONTACT: Bureau of Land Management, El Malpais Ranger Station, 505-280-2918, blm.gov/visit/el-malpais-nca

OPEN: Year-round

SITES: 10

EACH SITE HAS: Shade structure and picnic table on a concrete pad, fire ring with grill and a pedestal grill.

WHEELCHAIR ACCESS: None

ASSIGNMENT: First-come, first-served; no reservations

REGISTRATION: None

FACILITIES: 2 vault toilets

PARKING: At sites

FEE: Free.

ELEVATION: 6,454'

RESTRICTIONS

PETS: Dogs permitted on leashes; no horses

FIRES: In fire rings only

QUIET HOURS: 10 p.m.–6 a.m., including generators

ALCOHOL: Permitted at sites

OTHER: Maximum 8 people and 2 vehicles/site, including visitors; no holding a site; 7-day stay limit every 28 days; checkout at 2 p.m.; no fireworks. No collecting of wood, plants, rocks, animals, or natural/historical objects.

While the campground has an overall spacious feel, sites 6, 7, and 8 are fairly close together. Sites 2 and 5 afford the most privacy. Several sites have pull-through parking, which sets them farther from the road and creates more privacy. This small loop of campsites fills up quickly, so it's best to get here early to claim a spot. (*Note:* You cannot save a site for someone else.) The BLM makes it easy to become a camp host here by applying on their website, and there is one unnumbered host site with its own solar panels near the entrance.

Water is unavailable at the campground, but you can fill up at the ranger station between 8:30 a.m. and 4 p.m. They limit visitors to 5 gallons a day. In addition to bringing your own water, you should plan to bring your own firewood—or take a side trip into Grants to purchase some—because it is prohibited to gather firewood at Joe Skeen.

The park offers many opportunities to hike on, above, or under the lava flows. Several hikes take you across the lava. The mile-long Lava Falls Trail loop gives a good taste of hiking across the jagged basalt by following rock cairns. The rewarding Zuni-Acoma Trail, 7.5 miles one-way, will take you in the footsteps of Ancestral Puebloans as you follow rock cairns and walk across lava bridges still in use from the ancient route. You will likely want to set up a shuttle car at the end of the trail or plan to hike part of the way before turning back. Leave any pottery sherds where you find them.

The closest highlight to the campground is La Ventana Natural Arch, an arch carved in Jurassic Zuni sandstone. The viewing point for the arch is accessed by an 0.25-mile trail from the parking lot; it is best photographed in the late afternoon. Sandstone Bluffs Overlook, just north of the campground, affords a stunning, panoramic view of the lava flows. The 9-mile Narrows Rim Trail leads you up a sandstone bluff with wonderful scenic views of the flows and La Ventana.

Many lava tubes and ice caves lie beneath the flows near NM 53; to explore them, you will need a free caving permit from the El Malpais Visitor Center (the one at Exit 85 off I-40) and the proper equipment. Because lava rock is porous, rainfall permeates it easily; the lava rock also insulates the water, preventing evaporation—this rainfall then cools to become ice. In Giant Ice Cave, in the Big Tubes area, columns of crystalline ice can grow several feet high. A much easier cave to access and explore is Junction Cave in the El Calderon area. June–September, you can sign up for a ranger-guided evening hike to watch thousands of Brazilian free-tailed bats swirl out of the caves on the hunt for insects.

El Malpais National Conservation Area: Joe Skeen Campground

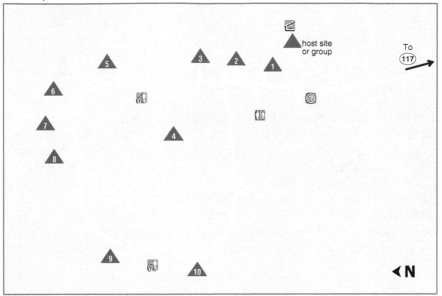

GETTING THERE

From I-40 Exit 89 (Quemado) just east of Grants, drive south on NM 117 for 11 miles. The campground will be on the left. *Note:* If there is water in the arroyo, the BLM recommends that you wait until it dissipates before crossing.

GPS COORDINATES: N34° 56.463' W107° 49.427'

45

⛺ El Morro National Monument Campground

Beauty ★★★★★ Privacy ★★★ Spaciousness ★★★ Quiet ★★★★★ Security ★★★★ Cleanliness ★★★★

Join seven centuries of visitors when you camp at El Morro.

Passersby have visited El Morro, "The Headland," for centuries; until 1906, when it became a national monument, many left their mark on the rock. A small, shaded oasis, surrounded by cattails, enticed many travelers to camp and refill their water here. From ancient, pecked petroglyphs and notes carved by conquistadores to the etched names and visiting dates of Americans, history and culture come together at El Morro. Some of the 2,000 carvings show humor; some are written as poems. Quite a few look like professional engravers took their chisels to the rock. Two of the most famous signatures are those of conquistador Don Juan de Oñate, who wrote "Paso por aqui" (the 17th-century Spanish equivalent of "I was here") on April 16, 1605, and Don Diego de Vargas, who recorded the 1692 reconquest of New Mexico after the Pueblo Revolt.

Camping here places you within a historical timeline of visitors, but the campground, a little ways away from the monument, is much more modern and developed than those in the 17th century. Most of the sites are well shaded by one-seed juniper and piñon. They are equipped with picnic tables, fire rings with grills, and level gravel tent pads. There is a double (men's and women's) vault toilet, outside of which you'll find a topography map of the area.

El Morro, easily visible from the plains, has been a destination and a layover for centuries.

KEY INFORMATION

LOCATION: NM 53, Ramah, NM 87321

CONTACT: El Morro National Monument, 505-783-4226, ext. 801, nps.gov/elmo

OPEN: Year-round

SITES: 9

EACH SITE HAS: Picnic table, fire ring, gravel tent pad

WHEELCHAIR ACCESS: Site 5; accessible toilets

ASSIGNMENT: First-come, first-served; no reservations

REGISTRATION: Self-register on-site

FACILITIES: Vault toilet, water spigots, visitor center nearby

PARKING: At sites

FEE: Free

ELEVATION: 7,160'

RESTRICTIONS

PETS: Permitted on leash except in the visitor center

QUIET HOURS: 10 p.m.–6 a.m.

FIRES: In fire rings and camp stoves only

ALCOHOL: Permitted at sites

OTHER: 14-night stay limit; maximum 8 people, 2 vehicles, and 2 tents/site; using a metal detector is prohibited. The park asks that you remain within 150 feet of the road.

Sites 1, 2, and 3 are very close together. That said, site 1 is lovely and not as sandwiched as the sites next to it. Site 9 has the most space and privacy; it's set back from the road a little more. Site 5 is accessible, and the campground asks that it be occupied only by someone who needs it. In addition to the fire ring and picnic table, site 5 is paved and has its own water fountain. The toilet, trash, and recycling bins sit across the road from this site.

In the middle of the ring road, there is an amphitheater with several benches and a fire pit, where evening talks are presented throughout the summer. Water spigots (between sites 1 and 2, 6 and 7, and at site 5) are dispersed through the campground, but once nighttime temperatures fall below freezing, they are shut off for the season. While the campground is free, the park still asks that you register your stay by filling out a form at the bulletin board by site 1.

From the visitor center, a lovely 2-mile hike guides you to the inscriptions and petroglyphs. If you continue up the sandstone cuesta, the trail will lead you to the ruins of Atsinna Pueblo. (*Atsinna* is a Zuni place-name meaning "a place of writings on the rock.") Along the trail, piñon jays swoop from Gambel oaks to saltbrush. The beautiful and bizarre fetid goosefoot turns bright red in autumn, looking like an out-of-place coral. Switchbacks take you to the top of the bluff (250′ of elevation gain), and the trail morphs into a carved outline with steps chiseled directly into the rock. The rolling, petrified sand dunes at the top (Zuni sandstone) change from white to pastel reds and oranges. A breathtaking 360° view shows the Zuni Mountains, the El Malpais lava fields, and the El Morro valley. Only a portion of the ruins has been unearthed—the rest remain buried to preserve them—but they are a nice climax to this hike.

If you're looking for other attractions in the area, Tuesday–Sunday you can book a tour of the Wild Spirit Wolf Sanctuary. Displaced, unwanted, and unreleasable captive-bred wolves, wolf-hybrid dogs, and foxes have found a lifelong home at this sanctuary. From El Morro, continue on NM 53, take BIA 125 south for 8 miles, and then take the right fork on BIA 120. The sanctuary will be 4 miles farther, on the left. Zuni Pueblo, farther west on NM 53, also has a number of attractions; a great visitor center will point you toward ruins, hiking, and many art galleries—80% of Zuni families are involved in making some type of art.

The closest towns for conveniences are Grants (42 miles to the east) and Black Rock (31 miles to the west). However, you can fill up with gas at the Lewis Trading Post, about 8 miles west of the park on NM 53.

El Morro National Monument Campground

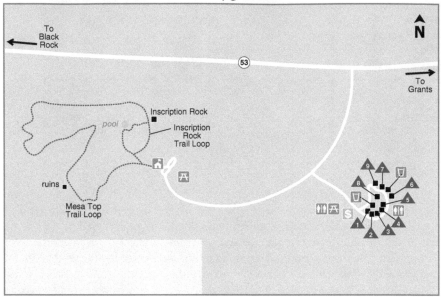

GETTING THERE

From Grants, take I-40 Exit 81 for NM 53 South. In 41 miles, the entrance for the monument will be on the left (south) side of the road, and the campground turnoff will be on your left, before you reach the visitor center.

GPS COORDINATES: N35° 02.208' W108° 20.268'

46

⚑ Gila Cliff Dwellings National Monument Campgrounds

Beauty ★★★★★ Privacy ★★★★ Spaciousness ★★★★ Quiet ★★★★★ Security ★★★★ Cleanliness ★★★★

At Gila Cliff Dwellings National Monument, pitch your tent at the doorstep of history, spending your days exploring the ruins and your evenings soaking in nearby hot springs.

Five cliff alcoves with interlinked dwellings form the ancient architecture that gives this national monument its name. At Gila Cliff Dwellings National Monument, you can pitch your tent at the doorstep of history, spending your days exploring incredible ruins and your evenings soaking in nearby hot springs. Upper and Lower Scorpion Campgrounds start only a quarter mile from the monument entrance.

Following the stream that flows through the deep and narrow Cliff Dweller Canyon into the West Fork of the Gila River, you'll see shelters that have been dug out of the volcanic tuff, which naturally erodes over time. One cave, about as long and wide as a football field, holds apartment-style buildings, a plaza, and a circular kiva. The flat stones forming the masonry are joined to the rock; in some areas the rock ceiling is 30 feet high.

The people of the Mogollon culture are believed to have lived here around the mid-13th century; no one knows why they left. Archaeologists have identified 46 rooms, perhaps occupied by 10–15 families. These homes once contained pottery, small corn cobs, broken arrowheads, manos and metates, fragments of obsidian and flint, woven yucca fibers, and a mummy.

In more recent history, the first Anglos at the ruins stumbled across the site while hiding in the hills to evade jury duty in 1878. In the decades that followed, a resort popped up at nearby Gila Hot Springs, and the owners led tours through the dwellings. In an effort to preserve the

Gila Cliff Dwellings is the only unit in the National Park System to contain Mogollon sites.

KEY INFORMATION

LOCATION: NM 15, just outside of Gila Cliff Dwellings National Monument

CONTACT: Gila National Forest, Wilderness Ranger District, 575-536-2250, tinyurl.com/upperscorpion, tinyurl.com/lowerscorpion

OPEN: Year-round

SITES: 17 in 2 campgrounds

EACH SITE HAS: Picnic table, fire ring

WHEELCHAIR ACCESS: None

ASSIGNMENT: First-come, first-served; no reservations

REGISTRATION: Self-register on-site

AMENITIES: Vault toilet; visitor center has water

PARKING: Paved parking area

FEE: Free

ELEVATION: 5,712'

RESTRICTIONS

PETS: Permitted on leash, except in enclosed buildings

QUIET HOURS: 10 p.m.–6 a.m.

FIRES: In fire rings only

ALCOHOL: Permitted at sites

OTHER: 14-day stay limit; not conducive to RV camping; no ATVs/OHVs; hunting and target practice prohibited

site and halt artifact removal, President Theodore Roosevelt established the Gila Cliff Dwellings as a national monument through executive proclamation on November 16, 1907.

To visit the namesake ruins, you'll hike a mile-long loop with several footbridges over the stream. It takes about an hour to walk. In addition to the ruins, camping here allows access to miles of great trails and hot springs. This is the country's first nationally designated wilderness area, and it has more than 870 square miles of forest to explore—and plenty of dark sky for stargazers.

Upper and Lower Scorpion Campgrounds are just outside the national monument. The West Fork of the Gila River runs alongside the campgrounds. Narrowleaf cottonwood, Arizona sycamore, and Arizona alder grow along the riverbanks—as does poison ivy. In some areas, you may encounter wild grapes near the river. It's easy to imagine ancient peoples tilling the riverside to grow squash, corn, and beans. Tall cliffs rise as a lovely, sunlit backdrop for both campgrounds.

Upper Scorpion Campground, the closest to the cliff dwellings, has 10 walk-in sites, all situated around a shared parking lot. Each site has a picnic table and fire pit; a vault toilet is accessible from the parking lot.

Lower Scorpion Campground is about half a mile from the national monument. It has seven developed sites, each with a picnic table and fire ring. You have to carry your provisions a short distance from your car to your campsite. This campground is a little more uneven than the larger Upper Scorpion; the flatter sites are closest to the toilets.

Neither campground is suitable for RVs. Potable water and trash bins are available at the Gila Cliff Dwellings visitor center. Please pack out any trash and help keep the area beautiful by picking up any you see along the river.

Short and accessible, Trail to the Past 173 meanders from the campground to a two-room cliff dwelling with pictographs. It does not connect with West Fork Trail 151, which skirts the campgrounds and cliff dwellings before heading off into the wilderness. The full trail is 34.5 miles and is most popular in the summer when the dry weather makes the scores of river crossings easier. The Grudging cabin and the cliff dwelling at mile 3.1 make great destinations for a day hike.

If you'd rather soak in warm water after exploring the ruins, you're in luck: there are two hot springs nearby. Lightfeather Hot Springs is a 20-minute hike from the visitor center, down Middle Fork Trail 157. The 130°F water pulses from the ground about once a minute and flows into the Middle Fork of the Gila River. The very popular Jordan Hot Springs is about 6 miles from the visitor center via Little Bear Canyon. These hot springs run about 94°F, and the pool is 20 feet wide and 3 feet deep.

Two other campgrounds are nearby if you strike out by the monument: Forks Campground (7 sites) is also on NM 15, about 5 miles from the visitor center, just north of the Gila River Bridge; Grapevine Campground (20 sites) is just south of the Gila River Bridge. Neither has tables or grills, but they do have vault toilets, and the camping is free of charge.

About 4 miles south of the campgrounds, you can find gas, groceries, and fishing licenses at Doc Campbell's General Store; hot-springs showers are also available for a fee. For all other services, the closest towns are Mimbres (an hour drive) and Silver City (2 hours)—both require traversing the twisting Trail of the Mountain Spirits Scenic Byway again, so it's best to double-check your supplies before heading into the wilderness.

Gila Cliff Dwellings National Monument Campgrounds

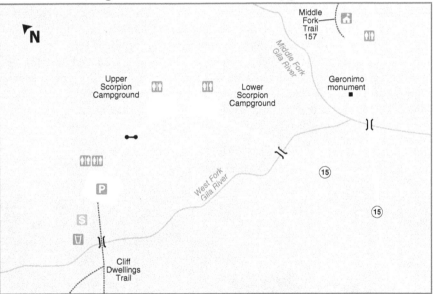

GETTING THERE

From the intersection of US 180 and NM 15 in Silver City, take NM 15 North for 43 miles. Follow the signs to Gila Cliff Dwellings National Monument; the campgrounds are on the right (north) side of the road, just before the visitor center. *Note:* The trip takes approximately 2 hours due to the winding mountain road.

GPS COORDINATES:
  Upper Scorpion Campground N33° 13.842' W108° 15.652'
  Lower Scorpion Campground N33° 13.815' W108° 15.468'

47

Juniper Campground

Beauty ★★★ Privacy ★★ Spaciousness ★★ Quiet ★★ Security ★★★★ Cleanliness ★★★★

A favorite of fishermen and hunters, Juniper Campground is a scenic place to rest after a day on the lake or in the forest.

In the northern reaches of Gila National Forest, deep shadows, long vistas, and high peaks abound. As the cottonwood and willow change colors in the autumn, the drive along NM 32 between Quemado and Apache Creek becomes increasingly beautiful. Quemado Lake sits in the middle of this scenic drive, straddling lush riparian and piñon–juniper woodland ecosystems. In the summer, the climate is mild and dry, with pleasantly cool nights. Monsoon showers in July and August are fleeting. Walking through the forest, you might catch a glimpse of deer, pronghorn, elk, javelinas, black bears, mountain lions, or wild turkeys.

Constructed in 1971, Quemado Lake is a 130-acre recreation reservoir nestled in the mountains. Right up the road from the lake are Juniper, Piñon, and El Caso Campgrounds. The New Mexico Department of Game and Fish (NMDGF) stocks Quemado Lake with rainbow trout and tiger muskie. In the 1990s, the lake became overrun with goldfish—one count, in 1999, found 70,000 mature fish. Seventy tons of goldfish (over 500,000 individual fish) have since been mechanically removed the lake (the seemingly unreal numbers may be attributed to anglers using the fish as bait). The NMDGF introduced tiger muskie as a form of biological control to keep the goldfish population in check. This plan appears to be working: it's now easier to catch trout because they aren't being eaten by goldfish first, and periodic analyses of tiger muskie stomachs reveal fewer goldfish, indicating a population in decline. Will the tiger muskie move on to devouring trout? Only time will tell.

Junipers and pines create some privacy at this campground.

KEY INFORMATION

LOCATION: FS 13, Quemado, NM 87829

CONTACT: Gila National Forest,
Quemado Ranger District, 575-773-4678,
tinyurl.com/junipercampground

OPEN: May 1–September 30

SITES: 17 tent sites

EACH SITE HAS: Picnic table, pedestal grill,
and fire ring

WHEELCHAIR ACCESS: Sites 21 and 30;
accessible toilets

ASSIGNMENT: First-come, first-served;
some sites can be reserved by calling
the ranger district above

REGISTRATION: Self-register on-site

AMENITIES: Drinking water, vault toilets

PARKING: At sites

FEE: $10/night single sites;
$16/night double sites
(50% discount with an Interagency Pass)

ELEVATION: 7,712'

RESTRICTIONS

PETS: Permitted on leash

FIRES: In fire rings only

ALCOHOL: Permitted at campsites only

OTHER: 14-day stay limit; 35' RV limit

While you can fish for trout (the NMDGF stocks 30,000 catchable trout each year), the tiger muskie is designated as catch-and-release while it continues to feed on unwanted fish. You may, however, take one tiger muskie home—if it's over 40 inches long.

On a rise above Quemado Lake, Juniper Campground has a nice view of the water as well as the nearby peaks. Sites 1–18 form the RV park, while 19–36, the tent-camping spots, are on a loop of their own. Some RVs may claim sites in the tent loop, but there's no electricity for them, and the parking areas tend to be too small for their rigs. Site 20 has its own little footpath down to the lake. Sites 21 and 30 are accessible for those in wheelchairs.

Each site has a defined area of crushed gravel to pitch your tent, a charcoal pedestal grill, a fire ring, and a picnic table. Pine and juniper trees border many of the sites, offering a little extra privacy. Some sites have level dirt patches under the trees so you can pitch your tent in the shade. The sites all sit near the gravel road, though, so it can get dusty when the wind picks up or when cars drive quickly down the road. You may also hear traffic noise from Forest Service Road 13, particularly on busy summer days.

Two composting toilets sit at either end of the tent loop; you'll also find trash bins there. Four water spigots are spaced throughout the loop. Don't clean fish, cookware, or yourself at the water pumps—the camp host forbids it, and it would attract bears. A previous edition of this book said you could pay for a shower at Snuffy's Steakhouse and Cowboy Saloon, a mile west of the campground. Snuffy's has since closed, but once a new business operates in the old bunkhouse, originally built in 1884, you might be able to shower there or stop in for beverages at the old antique bar.

The town of Quemado is 21 miles from Piñon and Juniper Campgrounds, but there is nowhere in Quemado to purchase a fishing license. You can purchase a license at the Apache Creek Store, 25 miles south of Quemado Lake on NM 32. If you plan to fish, you'll need a license, as the area is frequently patrolled. At the Cove Day Use Area, there are boat ramps (for electric and nonmotorized boats only), two ADA-compliant fishing piers, and spigots of drinking water during the summer. You can canoe, kayak, paddleboard, raft, or row on the lake May 1–September 30; it is closed from early fall to late spring.

Fishing isn't the only pastime in Quemado—if you're up for an adventure, you can visit *The Lightning Field,* a Land Art masterpiece made by Walter De Maria in 1977. In the nearby desert, De Maria erected 400 stainless steel poles in a grid a mile wide and a kilometer long. From mid-July through August, in the heart of monsoon season, lightning storms light up the area. You don't need lightning to appreciate the scale and beauty of this work. To check it out, book in advance at diaart.org/exhibition/exhibitions-projects.

Juniper Campground

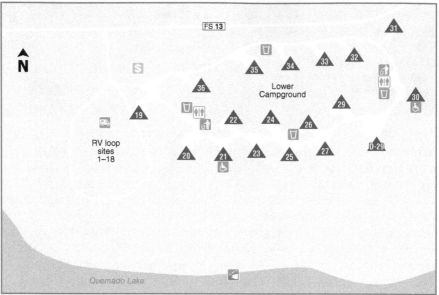

GETTING THERE

From the intersection of US 60 and NM 32 in Quemado, take NM 32 South 14 miles to Quemado Lake. Turn left (east) on NM 103, and after 4 miles, continue on gravel FS 13. The campground is 0.8 mile ahead, on the right.

GPS COORDINATES: N34° 08.250' W108° 29.345'

48

⛺ Piñon Campground

Beauty ★★★ Privacy ★★ Spaciousness ★★ Quiet ★★★ Security ★★★★ Cleanliness ★★★★

In the remote and scenic northern reaches of the Gila National Forest, you'll find many opportunities for relaxation and recreation at Piñon Campground.

Throughout the summer, you can grab a canoe and slip into Quemado Lake to spend the day paddling or fishing. The water levels of the lake may vary in drought years or after winters with low snow pack, but this 130-acre reservoir always provides pleasant opportunities for recreation. Families with paddleboards launch from the boat ramp. Anglers cast from the shores or the Cove Day Use Area. Many nice hikes leave from the lake and lead to commanding vistas of the valley. Three nearby campsites—Piñon, Juniper (see page 158), and El Caso—give you a place to rest after your adventure.

At Piñon Campground, piñon and Rocky Mountain juniper shade many of the sites. Lichen-covered rocks lay strewn in patchy grasses. Elk roam through the campground when fewer tents are set up. In the evenings, grab your binoculars and look for elk at the upper end of the lake, where the habitat is ideal for a sunset sighting. Use caution driving at night, as elk frequently walk on the roads.

A few sites have a view of Quemado Lake, but it's mostly hidden behind the pines. This lightly used campground—quieter than Juniper Campground and more developed than El Caso—has several tent sites to choose from.

Nonmotorized watercraft are welcomed on the waters of Quemado Lake.

KEY INFORMATION

LOCATION: FS 13, Quemado, NM 87829

CONTACT: Gila National Forest,
Quemado Ranger District, 575-773-4678,
tinyurl.com/pinoncampground

OPEN: May 1–September 30

SITES: 23 tent sites plus 2 group sites

EACH SITE HAS: Picnic table, pedestal grill,
and fire ring

WHEELCHAIR ACCESS: 2 sites;
accessible toilets

ASSIGNMENT: First-come, first-served;
no reservations

REGISTRATION: Self-register on-site.

AMENITIES: Drinking water, vault toilets,
RV dump station

PARKING: At sites

FEE: $10/night standard sites;
$35–$55/night group sites
(50% discount with an Interagency Pass)

ELEVATION: 7,880'

RESTRICTIONS

PETS: Permitted on leash,
except in enclosed buildings

QUIET HOURS: 10 p.m.–6 a.m.

FIRES: In fire rings only

ALCOHOL: Permitted at sites only

OTHER: 14-day stay limit

Just past the registration and host site, Piñon Campground divides into two loops—the right loop leads to two group sites that accommodate 30 people and 75 people; each has a pavilion with tables, charcoal grills, and fire rings. The left loop has 23 tent sites (numbers 37–59), all first-come, first-served. The hosts recommend that tent campers claim sites on the outside of the loop, leaving the inner sites for RVs to back into. RVs can fit in some of the sites, and there is a dump station for them at the entrance, but because the campground doesn't have electric hookups and parking isn't easy, most RV campers seem to prefer Juniper Campground. Two sites are accessible for those in wheelchairs.

On either end of the loop, there are composting toilets, trash bins, and water spigots. The water is safe to drink.

Each site has a defined area of crushed gravel to pitch your tent, a charcoal pedestal grill, a fire ring, and a picnic table. The sites all sit near the gravel road; although trees add some privacy, they don't protect you from the dusty road when it's windy. Next to site 47, the Piñon Access Trail, a 0.8-mile footpath, will take you down to the lake.

Fishing isn't the only pastime at Quemado Lake Recreation Area; there are several nearby hiking trails as well. Vista Trail 1 is a steep, high-elevation trail that cuts through ponderosa pines to a scenic vista. At the Quemado parking area, start hiking west on Lakeshore Trail to cross the dam (0.5 mile), and then connect to Overlook Trail. Follow the trail for 1 mile to the trailhead for Vista Trail. From the vista, you can see El Caso Peak, Castle Rock, and Largo Canyon. Alternatively, you could continue on Overlook Trail for more photographic angles, or connect to El Caso Lookout Trail or Sawmill Canyon Trail. None of the trails have potable water; make sure to bring enough for a steep, moderately difficult, high-elevation hike.

Horses are prohibited in Quemado Lake Recreation Area, but there is a "throwdown" area at the El Caso campsites nearby. El Caso I, II, III, and Throwdown lie farther down Forest Service Road 13 and to the right. These free campsites sit in a floodplain that connects to the lake and are more primitive than Piñon and Juniper Campgrounds. Popular with hunters, horsepackers, and large groups in the summer, the El Caso sites hosted several hunting parties with RVs playing loud music when I visited; otherwise, this campground had a lovely atmosphere. Cottonwoods and ponderosa pines provide shade, and a creek runs from the lake to the campground. Each campground is equipped with a toilet, but only El Caso I has a trash bin. The unnumbered sites have one picnic table and fire ring. The grass was knee-high at the unclaimed sites. Largo Trailhead 14 starts from the west of the campground and connects with other trails in the area.

Piñon Campground

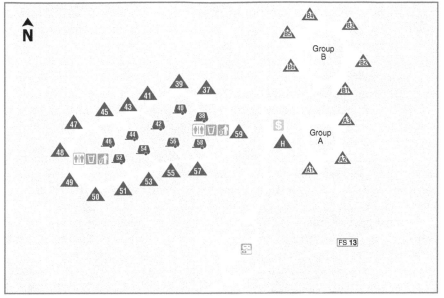

GETTING THERE

From the intersection of US 60 and NM 32 in Quemado, take NM 32 South 14 miles to Quemado Lake. Turn left (east) on NM 103, and after 4 miles, continue on gravel FS 13. The campground is 1.4 miles ahead, on the left.

GPS COORDINATES: N34° 08.286' W108° 29.013'

49

Pueblo Park Campground

Beauty ★★★★★ Privacy ★★★ Spaciousness ★★★★★ Quiet ★★★★★ Security ★★ Cleanliness ★★

Open and grassy, with many tall ponderosa pines, alligator junipers, and Emory oaks, Pueblo Park Campground is a cool, shady campground.

This campground has long been a favorite stop of mine in Gila National Forest. Open and grassy, with many tall ponderosa pines, alligator junipers, and Emory oaks, Pueblo Park Campground is a cool, shady campground. Mule deer browse the brush along the forest road; woodpeckers wake late-sleeping campers in their tents. At sunset the fading light adds a rosy hue to the bark of the ponderosa pines. Just outside of Reserve, it's perfectly situated to stage your entrance into the Gila, whether you're planning to investigate one of the many ghost towns nearby or head out for a hike. I once camped here in the late spring, and it was so cold that the ground froze and pushed tiny ice stalagmites up through the pine needles; inside my tent, my breath condensed and froze, becoming tiny snowflakes that flurried down, landing on my cheeks.

A loop and a spur make up the entirety of Pueblo Park Campground—around the loop, you'll find sites 1–6, somewhat close together; 7–10 along the spur have much more space between sites and long entry driveways. Site 4 is particularly nice, as it's set off from the first loop and very spacious. Thanks to the long parking spur and a ring of evergreens, site 9 has the most privacy and is a choice spot to pitch a tent. This site and others have large seats made from fallen ponderosa pines, but you will still want to bring camping chairs to get close to the fire.

Past site 10, the spur ends at two corrals. The information signs ask that horses not trot through the campground; the corrals open up to a trail on the back side. Along the back of site

Some sites have carved ponderosa thrones, but you'll want a camp chair to cozy up to the fire.

KEY INFORMATION

LOCATION: FS 232 near Reserve

CONTACT: Gila National Forest,
Reserve Ranger District, 575-533-6232,
tinyurl.com/pueblopark

OPEN: April–November

SITES: 10

EACH SITE HAS: Picnic table,
fire ring

WHEELCHAIR ACCESS: None

ASSIGNMENT: First-come, first served;
no reservations

REGISTRATION: Self-register in log

AMENITIES: Vault toilets, horse corrals,
interpretive trail

PARKING: At sites

FEE: Free

ELEVATION: 6,201'

RESTRICTIONS

PETS: Permitted on leash

QUIET HOURS: 10 p.m.–6 a.m.

FIRES: In fire rings only

ALCOHOL: Permitted at sites

OTHER: 14-day stay limit; no horses;
no shooting; 30' RV limit recommended
due to road conditions

9 and the corral, a large arroyo suggests either a roaring spring runoff or monsoon; many of the fence posts along the arroyo are secured with small boulders. Someone—perhaps the Civilian Conservation Corps or the U.S. Forest Service many years ago—collected several dozen smooth stones from the arroyo and used them to line pathways around the campground.

There is no trash service here—aside from a small trash can in each vault toilet, hardly large enough for waste produced one day at one campsite—so plan to pack out whatever you pack in. Additionally, Pueblo Park doesn't have water available; bring at least 5 gallons to drink, cook, clean, and dead-out your fire. The campground also does not have a dedicated camp host, but the Forest Service comes through regularly to attend to the area and restock and clean the restrooms. To register, sign your name in the logbook kept at the information kiosk near site 1.

The Trail to the Past, a nice interpretive trail that begins just beside site 6, walks you through prehistoric and historic settlement of the Pueblo Creek area. According to a brochure at the trailhead, this campground has been inhabited for 1,500 years—first by people of the Mogollon culture and much more recently by ranchers, miners, and the CCC. The trail is an easy mile and a half and will take about 2 hours if you stop to analyze each of the numbered posts.

Across the road from the campground, at the field where the CCC used to play softball during off-hours, the WS Mountain Trail 43 begins. This rugged canyon-bottom trail has 12 river crossings over the course of the 9 miles to WS Lake. You can access several other trails from this section of wilderness. If you head out for a hike, beware the many dangers that are common after forest Fires: loose or rolling rocks, falling trees or limbs, and flash floods.

In 1998, 11 Mexican wolves were released in the Blue Range Wilderness of the Apache National Forest (the northern edge of which is just across the road from the campground entrance) as part of a reintroduction program. More recently, captive-born wolf pups were placed in wild dens with the hopes that cross-fostering would add genetic diversity to the population. A 2018 count estimated that there are now 67 Mexican wolves in New Mexico (and more in Arizona); if you're lucky, you may hear them howling in the distance at night. While you're unlikely to see a wolf up close and personal, if you do, you can chase it away and then report the sighting to the U.S. Fish and Wildlife Service at 888-459-9653. Note that it's illegal to harm a wolf unless it's actually attacking a person; legally dogs don't count for such protection, so it's best to keep your canines close and leashed.

Reserve is the closest town to stock up on water and supplies, get a tire fixed, or grab an ice cream.

Pueblo Park Campground

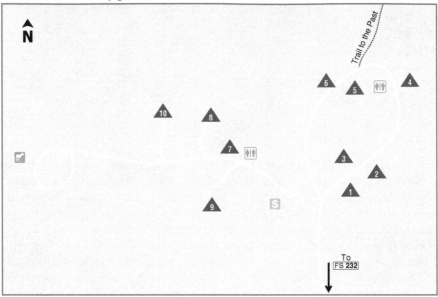

GETTING THERE

From the intersection of Main Street and NM 12 in Reserve, drive west on NM 12 for 7 miles; then turn left (south)onto US 180, and drive 4.7 miles to the Pueblo Park turnoff, on your right between mile markers 25 and 26. Continue right (east) on Forest Service Road 232 for 6 miles; the campground will be on your right.

GPS COORDINATES: N33° 35.596' W108° 57.685'

50

Water Canyon Campground

Beauty ★★★★ Privacy ★★★★ Spaciousness ★★★★ Quiet ★★★★ Security ★★ Cleanliness ★★★

This scenic getaway lies close to Socorro but has light usage most of the year.

In every direction you look, Water Canyon Campground presents beautiful views. To the northwest, there's the North Baldy (9,858′) obscuring Magdalena Peak (8,152′); to the south, South Baldy (10,783′), Timber Peak (10,510′), and Buck Peak (9,085′) peek above the canyon walls. La Jencia Basin is bisected by Water Canyon. The bench along the edge of the mountains is the Magdalena Fault, dividing the uplifted mountains from the plain below. The complex geological history of the Magdalena Mountains has created eye-catching formations and interesting scenery. They are named for Mary Magdalene, whose face is said to appear on the eastern slope of Magdalena Peak, in a talus formation dotted with shrubbery. From sites 7, 11, and 12, you can gaze down the canyon and glimpse the road you drove in on.

This pleasant, beautiful campground lies so close to Socorro that you'd expect it to get heavier traffic, but this scenic getaway has light usage most of the year. This may be in part due to the rocky, rutted gravel road, which is too narrow with turns too tight for many RVs.

You'll find a double (men's and women's) vault toilet and trash can at the entrance and again at the far side of the terminal loop; these toilets are ADA-accessible. Sites 1 and 8 are double sites. Site 11 feels a little exposed, but it has a great view. Site 9 has a spectacular view of the cliff, and it is surrounded by piñon and juniper trees.

At Water Canyon Campground, you might see faces in the cliffs; if you hike into the mountains, you might even recognize Mary Magdalene in the rocky slopes.

KEY INFORMATION

LOCATION: Water Canyon Road

CONTACT: Cibola National Forest
and National Grasslands,
Magdalena Ranger District,
575-854-2281, tinyurl.com/watercanyon

OPEN: April 1–November 1

SITES: 12

EACH SITE HAS: Picnic table, fire ring,
level tent area

WHEELCHAIR ACCESS: Accessible toilets

ASSIGNMENT: First-come, first-served;
no reservations

REGISTRATION: Self-register on-site

AMENITIES: Vault toilets, trash bins

PARKING: At sites

FEE: Free

ELEVATION: 6,926'

RESTRICTIONS

PETS: Permitted on leash

QUIET HOURS: 10 p.m.–6 a.m.

FIRES: In fire rings only

ALCOHOL: Allowed at sites

OTHER: 14-day stay limit;
the road is too narrow for large RVs

Alligator juniper dominates the woodland in the campground; interspersed are sotol, cholla, prickly pear, yucca, Apache plume, chamisa, and a variety of grasses. Many types of animals live in the mountains here, including mountain lions, black bears, pronghorn, mule deer, coyotes, red and gray foxes, bald and golden eagles, prairie falcons, kestrels, and Mearn's quail. At night you may hear the Mexican spotted owl hoot as it waits for woodrats to wander by.

At the picnic area, you'll notice a sign for Langmuir Laboratory. In 1980, Congress established this research site for atmospheric and astronomical study. Some 31,000 roadless acres were set aside for research, even though the area is not technically a wilderness. In part, the location was chosen because the mountains frequently create isolated, stationary, and small thunderstorms. Some of the campsites appear to suffer from runoff problems during these storms and monsoon rains, particularly site 6, which otherwise would be a nice, spacious area to camp in.

The group site, just down the rocky road from the campground (high-clearance vehicle recommended) is particularly nice. There are several parking spots, many spaces to pitch tents, and a big pavilion. While the site is marked as ADA-accessible, the parking lot alone would require an ATV wheelchair. To reserve the site, call the Magdalena Ranger District (575-854-2281). If it isn't reserved, the group site may be used for overflow camping. Otherwise, there are two other, small campgrounds nearby: Bear Trap Campground, on Old NM 52 South, has 4 sites and is 2 miles from Withington Lookout; Hughes Mill Campground, just a few miles past Bear Trap, has 2 sites and dispersed camping.

No camp host is assigned to Water Canyon Campground, but the U.S. Forest Service maintains the area and keeps the toilets and trash cans clean; if the trash cans fill, pack out your trash. No water is available here, so make sure to bring plenty for drinking, cooking, cleaning, and putting out your campfire. During the summer months, make sure to check fire restrictions before building your campfire—this area is hot and dry in the summer, and as such can be prone to fires.

If you have a sweet tooth, make sure to stop in nearby Pie Town to pick up a freshly baked pie from one of the many eateries along the highway. Pie Town also has roots in the livestock industry: an industrious baker named Clyde Norman, who made pocket-size apple pies for cowboys to eat while they drove cattle on to Magdalena, founded the town based on the reputation of his confections. Now only about 200 people live in Pie Town, but several bakeries line the highway and sell pies in both personal and shareable sizes. Each September, on the second Saturday of the month, the town hosts a Pie Festival, where bakers compete for the titles of Pie King and Queen. For anything more substantial than pie or a hearty breakfast, plan to stop in Socorro, 21 miles east.

Water Canyon Campground

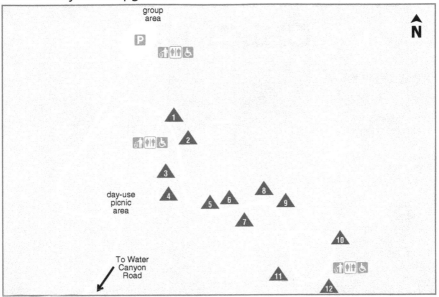

GETTING THERE

From Socorro, drive west on US 60 for about 15 miles. Then turn left (southwest) onto Water Canyon Road (you should see a sign for Water Canyon), and follow it 4.7 miles to the campground entrance, on the right at the fork where Water Canyon Road continues left.

GPS COORDINATES: N34° 01.539' W107° 07.835'

APPENDIX A

CAMPING EQUIPMENT CHECKLIST

GENERAL CAMP KIT

Batteries
Camp chairs
Extra tent stakes
Fire starters or matches
Firewood
Flashlight or headlamp
Insect-repellent candles
Lanterns (plus extra fuel if necessary)
Pillow
Sleeping bag
Sleeping pad
Tarp
Tent
Tent fabric sealant
Toilet paper

HEALTH AND HYGIENE KIT

First aid kit (see page 4)
Hand sanitizer
Prescription medications
Sun hat
Sunblock
Sunglasses
Toiletries (lip balm, Castile/biodegradable soap,
   deodorant, toothbrush, toothpaste, quick-drying
   towel, feminine products, wet wipes, etc.)

CAMP KITCHEN

5-gallon water container
Biodegradable dish soap, dish towel, scouring pad
Bowls and plates
Camp stove
Cookware (chopping knives, spatula, can opener,
   corkscrew, etc.)
Cooler
Cutting board
Eating utensils (forks, spoons, sporks, knives)
Extra bin for washing dishes
Extra propane
Foil

French press or coffeepot
Ice
Matches
Mugs
Olive oil, salt, pepper
Pot, skillet, and/or Dutch oven
Potholder
Trash bags

TOOL KIT

Cord or rope
Duct tape
Hatchet
Mallet or hammer
Multitool
Shovel

HIKING KIT

Bear spray
Bug spray
Glow sticks
GPS and/or compass
Topographic maps and/or trail maps
Water-purification tablets

RECREATIONAL KIT

Binoculars
Camera
Dog gear
Field guides and star charts, such as the following:
   *Field Guide to the Night Sky, National Audubon
   Society Field Guide to the Southwestern States,
   Roadside Geology of New Mexico,* and *Road-
   side History of New Mexico*
Hammock
Notebook and pen/pencil
Playing cards
Reading material
Solar charger
Sunshade
Tripod

APPENDIX B

SOURCES OF INFORMATION

The following is a partial list of agencies, associations, and organizations to contact for information on outdoor recreation opportunities in New Mexico.

U.S. FOREST SERVICE
fs.usda.gov

Carson National Forest
208 Cruz Alta Rd.
Taos, NM 87571
575-758-6200, fs.usda.gov/carson

Gila National Forest
3005 E. Camino del Bosque
Silver City, NM 88061
575-388-8201, fs.usda.gov/gila

Lincoln National Forest
3462 Las Palomas
Alamogordo, NM 88310
757-434-7200, fs.usda.gov/lincoln

Santa Fe National Forest
11 Forest Lane
Santa Fe, NM 87508
505-438-5300, fs.usda.gov/santafe

NATIONAL PARK SERVICE
nps.gov

Bandelier National Monument
15 Entrance Rd.
Los Alamos, NM 87544
505-672-3861, ext. 517

Chaco Culture National Historic Park
1808 CR 7950
Nageezi, NM 87037
505-786-7014, nps.gov/chcu

El Morro National Monument
Ramah, NM 87321
505-783-4226, ext. 801, nps.gov/elmo

White Sands National Park
Dunes Drive
Alamogordo, NM 88352
575-479-6124, nps.gov/whsa

BUREAU OF LAND MANAGEMENT
blm.gov

New Mexico State Office
301 Dinosaur Trail
Santa Fe, NM 87508
505-954-2000

El Malpais Ranger Station (Joe Skeen)
NM 117
Grants, NM 87020
505-280-2918, blm.gov/visit/el-malpais-nca

Las Cruces District Office (Aguirre Spring)
1800 Marquess St.
Las Cruces, NM 88005
575-525-4300

Socorro Field Office (Datil Well)
901 Old US 85 S.
Socorro, NM 87801
575-835-0412, blm.gov/office/socorro-field-office

Taos Field Office (Orilla Verde, Wild Rivers)
226 Cruz Alta Rd.
Taos, NM 87571
575-758-8851, blm.gov/office/taos-field-office

NEW MEXICO STATE PARKS
Headquarters
1220 S. St. Francis Dr.
Santa Fe, NM 87505
888-667-2757, emnrd.state.nm.us/SPD

U.S. ARMY CORPS OF ENGINEERS
Cochiti Lake Project Office
82 Dam Crest Road
Peña Blanca, NM 87041-5015
505-465-0307, www.spa.usace.army.mil
    /missions/civil-works/recreation/cochiti-lake

INDEX

U

V

W

Z

ABOUT THE AUTHOR

Amaris Feland Ketcham occupies her time with open space, white space, CMYK, flash nonfiction, long trails, f-stops, line breaks, and several Adobe programs running simultaneously. She has been camping, hiking, and exploring New Mexico for about 20 years. Her creative work has appeared in *Creative Nonfiction, The Kenyon Review, Rattle, Utne Reader,* and many more literary venues across the country. She has two books of poems published, *A Poetic Inventory of the Sandia Mountains* and *Glitches in the FBI*.

Amaris teaches interdisciplinary liberal arts at the University of New Mexico Honors College. Her courses include creative writing, nonfiction comics, place as text, and zines. She is the faculty advisor and instructor for the award-winning undergraduate literature and arts magazine, *Scribendi*.

Her work on Poetic Routes (poeticroutes.com) has been adopted by the Albuquerque City Planning Department as a way to use poetry as a means of understanding neighborhoods and community character and values throughout town. As a practitioner of creative placemaking, she has taught poetry workshops in Albuquerque's bosque and Place as Text Institutes with the National Collegiate Honors Council. Amaris has painted murals throughout Albuquerque, acted in a radio drama about Badlands National Park, and taken students on multiweek camping trips along the Lewis and Clark Trail.

DEAR CUSTOMERS AND FRIENDS,

SUPPORTING YOUR INTEREST IN OUTDOOR ADVENTURE, travel, and an active lifestyle is central to our operations, from the authors we choose to the locations we detail to the way we design our books. Menasha Ridge Press was incorporated in 1982 by a group of veteran outdoorsmen and professional outfitters. For many years now, we've specialized in creating books that benefit the outdoors enthusiast.

Almost immediately, Menasha Ridge Press earned a reputation for revolutionizing outdoors- and travel-guidebook publishing. For such activities as canoeing, kayaking, hiking, backpacking, and mountain biking, we established new standards of quality that transformed the whole genre, resulting in outdoor-recreation guides of great sophistication and solid content. Menasha Ridge Press continues to be outdoor publishing's greatest innovator.

The folks at Menasha Ridge Press are as at home on a whitewater river or mountain trail as they are editing a manuscript. The books we build for you are the best they can be, because we're responding to your needs. Plus, we use and depend on them ourselves.

We look forward to seeing you on the river or the trail. If you'd like to contact us directly, visit us at menasharidge.com. We thank you for your interest in our books and the natural world around us all.

SAFE TRAVELS,

BOB SEHLINGER
PUBLISHER